T.R.I.A.L.S.

"A Journey from Anxiety to Peace"

Chase Turner

SUNSET
INSTITUTE PRESS
3710 34th Street ❖ Lubbock, Texas
806/788/3280/1 ❖ Extschool@sibi.cc

Table of Contents

ACKNOWLEDGMENTS

Without a doubt, God and His word are the root of the material in this book. If the contents are able to help anyone overcome stress and anxiety, to God be the glory. I'm honored and blessed that anyone would consider reading my thoughts on this topic.

To my parents, thank you for providing me with direction, an example and an understanding of the role God plays in the human existence. I am a product of my upbringing.

To my beautiful wife and family, I pray that my daily example reflects the mindset needed to live without anxiety. My life is blessed and made easier because of your love and encouragement. I love you more than you know!

To you dear reader, if you are battling clinically diagnosed anxiety, the content in this book is not intended to shame you nor make you believe the diagnosis was your choice, neither is the content intended or designed to help you cure a clinical diagnosis of anxiety. If you need medical help for circumstances you are dealing with, please reach out to those who are able to help you. You are not alone, nor do you have to face this struggle alone. If you would like prayers, my email is chase@trialsbook.com. You can email me anytime and I will stop what I'm doing and pray for you. I hope as you read this material, the principles within the book will guide you in your relationships and help you to avoid adding more stress or anxiety in your daily walk.

For those who have not been diagnosed with anxiety but struggle with feeling anxious about your daily life, I ask you to read with an open mind and a willingness to accept that you are in control of much in this struggle. May God grant you the wisdom and courage that gives you the ability and desire to choose vulnerability and faith over anxiety. You can do it! I will be praying for you as you begin this journey.

FORWARD

June 10, 2019

How do you prepare for an opportunity of this magnitude? To say I am proud is an understatement. To say I am blessed is inadequate. To say I am thankful is deficient. Few fathers have the honor and, at the same time, the challenge of expressing what is indescribable and immeasurable. Chase's example, as described in this book, inspires everyone who knows him to improve in every area of life. His ability to take everyday situations that often result in stress and anxiety, while sharing common-sense solutions, only highlights the significance of his example even further.

As his father, I can think of no greater privilege than recommending this book to you. From the first chapter to the last, you will find it difficult to put down. Each chapter describes a specific area that creates stress and often leads to anxiety. Stress is inevitable, but how we deal with stress makes the difference. In order to deal with stress appropriately, Chase developed the T.R.I.A.L.S. method. Throughout these pages, he demonstrates how the T.R.I.A.L.S. method works to approach stress and overcome anxiety.

Unlike books that only focus on statistics, philosophy, or scientific data, T.R.I.A.L.S. represents the life of a man that consistently lives what he has written. His life is a testimony to the value of the method he has developed. I have watched Chase grow and develop as a Christian, husband, and father. I have witnessed him successfully approach every area of life by applying the T.R.I.A.L.S. method. You will benefit in the same way.

On a personal note, after reading T.R.I.A.L.S., I began to make application in my own life. I was amazed at the relevance found in each word. I can say with confidence that regardless of your age, gender, marital status, occupation, educational background, or social position, this book will help you. You will be blessed as you read because the foundation is biblical, the information is real, the illustrations are true, and the application provides practical ways to address the challenges of stress and eliminate anxiety.

Enjoy!

Bob Turner (dad)

Introduction to T.R.I.A.L.S.

If I told you the power of leaving anxiety behind and having positive, joy-filled days was as easy as reading this short book, would you believe me? No worries, I wouldn't either. However, I hope you will join me on a journey to see if you can convince yourself anxiety is a choice that we all have the power to choose to endure or let go.

So many areas in our life cause us anxiety, stress, worry, depression, etc. When we consider all the trigger points for these challenges we face, we must find the root or the core of what brings all these negative feelings and emotions. One of the underlying struggles we all deal with is the desire to be normal. We never want others to look at us and think we aren't "normal" or better put "like them" (from our own perspective). When we look at the world around us, don't we find the biggest group of people who seem to be similar, and then we try to be like them because they are the "normal" ones? It feels silly just saying those words, but so many live by them. Do we really want to be like everyone else?

Living without anxiety is a biblical concept and should be a reality for all of us. In Matthew 6:25 – 34, Jesus gives a mini-sermon on anxiety in life. Six times in these few verses we see the word "worry." If someone ever had cause for worry or anxiety in life, Jesus was a prime candidate. Knowing in advance what He was going to suffer, He still chose the path of the cross. These are the credentials needed for commanding us not to worry. The context in which this was written is certainly different from our world today, but there is still much application to be made to help us overcome the anxiety that accompanies the daily decisions we are forced to make. Jesus says not to be anxious about food, clothing, and time, but the application is not limited to just these three areas. If we make practical application of this command, we should include food, clothing, time, cars, housing, and so many other things surrounding us today.

The apostle Paul is another author who has the credentials for writing about living life without worry. While writing his letter to the church in Philippi, he is in prison in Rome waiting to learn if he would be executed or released. He says in Philippians 4:6 – 7, "Be anxious for nothing, but in everything with prayer and supplication, let your requests be made known to God and the peace that surpasses all comprehension will guard your hearts and minds in Christ Jesus."

Let the first few words sink in, "be anxious for nothing." How many of us have genuinely tried to put these words into practice? How many of us have experienced success in the process? As far as application goes, these could be some of the most challenging words we read in the Bible!

If nothing else, I hope we commit this verse to memory as we learn how to reduce stress and eliminate anxiety in our lives. This verse has become the mantra or guide for my life, and I hope it encourages you to know you don't have to live with anxiety. For many of us, in our pursuit to be normal, we have placed a tremendous amount of stress on ourselves. We live in a world that promotes stressful living. The culture we live in dictates what our desires and needs should be, and, for some reason, we listen. Why? The simplest answer is INSECURITY. We will look at this idea in more detail in the pages ahead, but the idea is the opposite of contentment. Too often we accept as a fact that anxiety is inevitable. We are taught we should learn how to live with it instead of how to prevent it. We live on the go and life moves so fast we aren't always sure which end is up. The less time we *perceive* we have, the more stress we place on ourselves to accomplish everything on our to do list.

In *The Chronicles of Narnia, The Magician's Nephew* C. S. Lewis writes, "What you see and what you hear depends a great deal on where you are standing. It also depends on what sort of person you are." There is much truth in these few words from Lewis, especially the last sentence. Who we are determines where we stand. Do we really know who we are? If we don't, it is difficult to know where we stand. This confusion about, or lack of confidence in, who we are has the potential to cause instability and stress in our lives.

Wayne Walter Dyer was an American philosopher, self-help author, and motivational speaker. His first book, *Your Erroneous Zones*, is one of the best-selling books of all time, with an estimated 35 million copies sold to date. He is known for saying, "Change the way you look at things and the things you look at change" (Dyer). Do we want our circumstances or surroundings to change? Perhaps if we change the way we look at them, they will change on their own. This is a fundamental principle we will thread through each aspect of this book: Growth requires change.

> *"Change the way you look at things and the things you look at change" –* Wayne Walter Dyer

The bottom line when it comes to anxiety is this; it is a choice. If you have ever met someone who appeared to have little stress, perhaps none at all, I imagine you had one of two thoughts:

1. What a phony! This is the most pretentious person I have ever met! There is no way they don't have any anxiety!

    Probably a lot of people are like this. They put on a show when they are in public, but in their mind, they are completely lost. They may have an intense amount of anxiety from home life, work, financial struggles, etc., but you would never know because they hide their anxiety well.

2. Man, I wish I could be like them! I wish I didn't have anxiety in my life!
    > Believe it or not, there are people like this. Some people deal with stress in a way that does not cause them anxiety. This needs to be our goal.

Perception is key. What one person perceives as stress may not look like stress to a neighbor. In the first chapter, we will discuss the difference between stress and anxiety. This will allow us to understand the point of view we must have to avoid the potential mental and sometimes physical disasters that come because of self-inflicted stress.

The goal of achieving happiness and success goes hand in hand with having minimal amounts of stress and anxiety in your life. An abundance of research shows us how stress affects us internally, externally, financially, within our marriage, within our job, how we raise our kids, our faith, and the way we grieve. In all my reading, I've learned you can find research on both sides of nearly every subject to support whichever truth you choose to believe. Most of it is subjective. Because the bulk of my reading indicated most research is inconclusive, I decided not to include it in this book. I prefer not to view myself or others as a statistic. Statistics are not personal, but we are personal. I don't want us to compare ourselves to others to see which statistic defines us. Instead, I want to share with you what has worked for me and my family and how we have reduced stress in our life. I hope our solution can help you in your battle against fear, anxiety, and stress that may be plaguing your daily walk.

The happiest and most successful people are those who serve others. I would be remiss if I didn't thread my faith throughout this book because it is my belief in something much, much greater than myself that allows me to live with very little stress and no anxiety. Bar none, Jesus Christ is the most encouraging and successful leader in the world. Whether you believe in God or not, it is difficult to deny the impact Jesus and His teachings continue to have today, some 2,000 years after He walked the earth.

To the best of my ability, I have tried to live my life trusting in God to take care of me and my family while I, with His help, guide the ship of life we are privileged to sail. When we find ourselves meeting the needs of our family, church members, and friends, we discover helping others address stress in their lives eases some of our own anxiety.

The T.R.I.A.L.S. method has helped me in my journey to help others reduce stress in their life. I have developed this acronym hoping to help us all find practical ways to overcome stressful situations and anxiety.

T. = Transparency

R. = Responsibility

I. = Intentionality

A. = Appreciation

L. = Limits

S. = Simplify

At the end of each section, we will look at practical ways to implement these principles to reduce your current stress levels. Understanding T.R.I.A.L.S. has the potential to bring a tremendous amount of joy to your life. I encourage you to have an open mind and be optimistic about the possibility of reducing much of your stress and eliminating anxiety from your daily routine. The power to choose lies within you!

Questions to consider:

Which of the actions in the T.R.I.A.L.S. method is hardest for you? Why?

Which of the actions in the T.R.I.A.L.S. method is easiest for you? Why?

Chapter 1 – What Is stress and Where Does it come From?

When I was a kid, I loved reading Archie comics. I can remember going to garage sales when we lived in Canada and finding a box of Archie comics for $.25 each. I bought the entire box. It seemed like everyone I knew in school was one of the characters. I wasn't sure which character I was, but I knew I wanted to be Moose. I wanted to be tall, I wanted to have big muscles, and I wanted to have a little girlfriend I could carry around with one arm, should I so choose. I wanted to be attractive and overly self-confident. At an early age, I (unknowingly) put unrealistic expectations on myself because the goals I set required elements outside my control. While I could control self-confidence, I learned quickly the other goals I set determined my level of self-confidence. However, my height, weight, and getting the little girlfriend were not in my control. I also put stress on others I hadn't even met yet! Without realizing it, most of us place stress on ourselves at a very early age.

The older I get, I desperately want to say living without stress and anxiety gets easier, but unfortunately it still requires a great amount of effort. This past year, I was asked to speak at a lectureship in Minnesota. If you continue reading, you will see I strive to live a very minimalistic lifestyle. Because the lectureship was on a Saturday, I flew in Friday night and planned to fly back Sunday afternoon. To avoid checking a bag, I put my suit on a hanger and carried a back pack with all my essentials. When I woke up Saturday morning, my pants were not there! They had fallen off the hanger somewhere in the plane or airport, and I was left with a suit jacket and the jeans I wore on the plane. I began to think of all the possibilities of where my pants were, but it really didn't matter because there was no way to retrieve them prior to speaking. I then began to think about what everyone else would think of me speaking in jeans and a suit jacket and the stress began to grow and grow.

Sadly, I began to pretend I could read everyone's mind who attended. I knew exactly what they were going to think of me, or so I thought. I placed so much value on their opinions, and I didn't even know them. I imagine we have all done this at some point in our lives.

While most dictionaries define stress as pressure or tension exerted on something or a state of mental or emotional strain or tension resulting from adverse or very demanding circumstances, they don't mention one crucial factor: the origin of the pressure or tension. Why? For most people, the list would be so long it would require volumes of books to include all the possibilities! The reason we would have such long and different lists is because of circumstance and perception.

I'm not going to tell you stress is all in your head, but isn't that where it is? Is it not pressure we place on ourselves to be a certain way, to accomplish a certain task, to be in a certain place, or to have certain things? Where does our perception originate if not in our head? One of the benefits of stress being in our heads is people can't see it unless we allow. Problems arise because it tends to create imposters of many of us. We become puppets controlled by our inner desire to make sure everyone thinks we have it all together.

Unfortunately, social media also play a large role in perpetuating false reality. How often is reality portrayed on Facebook, Instagram, Twitter, etc.? How many pictures do we take before we find the perfect smile? How many happy vacation snapshots do we show the world so everyone knows it was a perfect trip when the reality is two people in our family were sick half the time? I won't mention it also rained at the most inconvenient times, and I lost my temper with my four-year-old because he or she was acting like a four-year-old. If we weren't so concerned with what others thought of all the choices we made and how good or bad our days were, how would we all fill our time?

Another debilitating attribute of this downward spiral we create within ourselves is it causes us to believe we don't have a choice. The inner turmoil created by our misguided psyche works against us until we explode. Sadly, these explosions tend to hurt us and those closest to us. Perhaps the worst part of it all is the explosion is not a solution to the problem, but merely a product.

> *"I have often wondered how it is that every man loves himself more than all the rest of men, but yet sets less value on his own opinion of himself than on the opinion of others" – Marcus Aurelius*

When we realize the power we have within us to control our reaction to circumstances, we can understand we don't have to live with anxiety. However, it also brings to life the unfortunate realization we choose to live with anxiety.

Where Does Stress Come From?

Contrary to popular belief, our reactions to stress are a choice, not something forced on us. One of the greatest struggles in life is the source of our stress. When we consider the choices we make every day, what are the greatest factors that influence us?

Roman emperor, Marcus Aurelius said, "I have often wondered how it is that every man loves himself more than all the rest of men, but yet sets less value on his own opinion of himself than on the opinion of others" (Meditations, Marcus Aurelius).

This thought paints a picture of a reality where most of us live. How sad to live each day giving permission to our friends, co-workers, church people, and the general public (whom we really don't know personally) to determine what we wear, how we wear it, what we say, and how we say it! They even influence our parenting, finances, exercise (if we exercise), and our food. The saddest truth in all of this is most people we give this power to don't care at all about what we are doing, eating, wearing, etc.

Most of us would admit to loving ourselves, at least to a certain extent. I know I would! I imagine we would also admit we are more concerned about what others think of us than what we think of ourselves. I would even be willing to bet, at times, we care more about the opinions of people we know and don't like more than we care about our own.

When we live like this, if we are not affirmed in the decisions we make, our self-esteem plummets. Low self-esteem is a trigger for our own negative perceptions. One of the keys to overcoming negative perceptions is confidence. In order for us to believe in ourselves, we have to find the ability to overcome the value we place on the opinions of others. Is it possible to wake up tomorrow and have less concern for what others think of us? Does thinking less of surrounding opinions create less stress in our lives? It is a step in the right direction. I'm not suggesting in any way we should be disrespectful to anyone, but we should have some respect and value of our own opinion. How we live teaches others so much about who we are, but our thoughts teach us the same lesson.

How would you fill in these statements?

I would have less stress if I had more _____.

I would have less stress if _____.

I run on the weekends with a couple of friends, and our conversations are never dull. I asked them to fill in these blanks, and I received two very different responses. One of

10

them said he would have less stress if he didn't volunteer for so much stuff. The other said he would have less stress if he wasn't married and didn't have children. I had to smile at both of their responses. They both admitted to being in control of their circumstances. Understanding how to overcome this stress fell within decisions they were capable of making. In case they ever read this book, I do have to say they are both happily married, and wouldn't trade their wives and kids for less stress. The point the second friend made was some stress comes from the pressure he places on himself while providing for and taking care of his family. It can be tough.

> "More of anything comes at the cost of something"

If we can fill in either of these blanks and know for certain we could eliminate some of the stress in our life, I would suggest some stress is voluntary. The key is filling in the blank with a realistic goal we can achieve to eliminate stress from our life. For example, if I say, "I would have less stress if I had more time," I must ask myself, "How can I have more time?" Because we all have the same amount of time, this requires sacrifice of time in a less stressful part of life so that we have more time to deal with the other areas of life that give us anxiety. We are in control of the areas we choose to worry about.

The two most common answers to these questions relate to our desire to have more time and money. The question then becomes, "How do I get more time and money?" If these become our focus, we will likely never be content. Every time we say yes to someone or something, we say no to someone or something else. More of anything comes at the cost of something. We must prioritize.

In regard to time management, I love how Mark Zuckerberg saves time on decisions that really aren't important. In an article posted on independent.co.uk/news website, the then 31-year-old was asked about why his outfits never changed. He said, "I really want to clear my life to make it so that I have to make as few decisions as possible about anything except how to best serve this community." He went on to say, "I'm in this really lucky position, where I get to wake up every day and help serve more than a billion people. And I feel like I'm not doing my job if I spend my energy on things that are silly or frivolous about my life." The article states Zuckerberg is worth an estimated $37.5 billion. Can you imagine being worth that much money and wearing a plain gray t-shirt to work every day?

Isn't it funny how stressful we make something as simple as picking out what to wear! Years ago, while I was getting ready to teach a Bible class at worship services on a Sunday morning, I thought, "Did I wear this last week?" What a blessing to come to the realization that it really didn't matter! I like to look nice, but our clothes are so insignificant. My concern for what others *might* think about what I wear from week to week at church should not be a factor in the way I view myself. Does it really matter to us how others dress? It shouldn't. It also shouldn't matter to us if someone cares about our clothes either.

In his book, _Rich Kid, Smart Kid_, Robert T. Kiyosaki talks about a meeting he had with Kathy Kolbe, the creator of the Kolbe Index. The Kolbe Index is a chart based on the target's answers to a series of questions to assess his or her instincts. Kolbe had very little information about Kiyosaki prior to their meeting. She had only read the results from his answers. During their conversation, she was able to deduce a great deal of information about him related to his childhood, his likes, dislikes, and how he preferred to learn. In the middle of their conversation, Kiyosaki asked her how she defined success. She responded, "I define success as the freedom to be yourself" (Kiyosaki). This is one of the great definitions that, when applied, will help us reduce stress in significant ways.

Success, or as Kolbe puts it "freedom to be yourself" means we are honest; honest with others and honest with ourselves. This is one of the hardest characteristics to develop because most of us have problems, but we keep them as secrets. Secrets cause anxiety. One of the blessings of being part of a family, community group, or the church is these groups exist to help us. However, we often put on a mask and answer the question "How are you today?" with the standard "I'm good, and you?" and move on to the next person. People aren't familiar with our problems, and we aren't familiar with theirs because we aren't open and honest with each other. I'm not suggesting we unload our burdens on a stranger or visitor, but we need people in our lives with whom we can share our burdens. Sounds scriptural, doesn't it? (Galatians 6:2).

Stress comes from many people, places, events, activities, sports, etc. What would happen if we choose to take control of our own lives? What if we choose to hold our own opinion of how we dress, work, raise our kids in a higher regard than the opinions of those around us? What if we choose to accept responsibility for the decisions we make? What if we choose to think before we act and speak? Is it possible we would enjoy life more if we understood we have the power to choose to do so? Power and freedom are synonymous when we look at this context. While there are obvious occasions in which we should choose to be respectful to others of how we present ourselves, we need to avoid being extreme to the point we have mental stress related to the perception others have of us.

Some people pass through life in constant stress and worry and occasionally, only occasionally, enjoy moments of pure joy and happiness. There are also others who live a joy-filled life, focusing on the positivity that exists around them while occasionally, only occasionally, feeling the stress and negative emotions that accompany the parts of life outside their control. My goal and hope are to help us all achieve the latter. May we all live with a joyful disposition, and the occasional discomfort of experiencing hardship that life sometimes presents us instead of living with constant negativity and the occasional moment of joy. It is much harder to enjoy the good times when we are surrounded by negativity. It's much easier to get through adverse circumstances when we use positivity as the lens though which we see life.

Bringing it Home

The way we act and the words we use allow those around us to see who we are on the outside. For most of us, a select few see our external life and our inner self as well. Usually, these people are around us on a regular basis. Whether it be a parent, spouse, child, or close friend, the unique bond created when we share our thoughts with others help us deal with the struggles this life presents us, and the way we choose to handle them.

It's amazing how small our bodies are in comparison to the size of our minds. We have big dreams, big thoughts, and aspirations in our mind. Often, we give our little bodies a small chance to succeed in carrying out our dreams because we aren't always realistic or because fear paralyzes us from starting the process. I'm not saying we shouldn't dream big; I believe we should. However, we should also have a good understanding of who we are, where we live, whom we live with and what our strengths and weaknesses are before we set out to make our dreams a reality.

Stress prevention begins with looking at potential trials that will come as a result of what and whom we surround ourselves with. Using the T.R.I.A.L.S. method helps prevent and reduce unnecessary stress in our lives, thus eliminating anxiety. Before making choices about education, marriage, family, jobs, finances, health, and faith, consider asking the following:

Transparency – Am I willing to be transparent with _____? Will _____ be transparent with me?

Responsibility – Am I willing to be responsible with _____? Will _____ be responsible with me?

Intentionality – What can I do to make sure I am intentional with _____?

Appreciation – Can I and will I appreciate _____? Will he or she appreciate me if I _____?

Limits – What will my limits be if I _____? Am I ok with these limits?

Simplify – How will _____ help me simplify things in my life so that I don't add stress?

We can fill in these blanks with several people, places, and things to help us understand the good, better, best choices in our future. I was taught as a kid if I failed to plan, then I planned to fail. If we want to reduce and prevent stress in our life, it won't happen by accident. We must make a plan, and we must stick to it. Let's use T.R.I.A.L.S. to help us and others overcome anxiety and stress, so we can be the best version of ourselves and live our best life.

The following nine chapters look at these questions in detail, and deal with a specific area of life along with the stress that often accompanies it. To help you on your journey, you will find a MAP at the end of each chapter to motivate, make application and a prayer for each day.

Chapter 2 – Life

I graduated from Freed Hardeman University, a private college in the little town of Henderson, Tennessee. These were four of the best years of my life, at least up to that point. I made the best friends during this time, and we still get together when we can although we would all agree it isn't often enough. During this time, my eyes were opened to the reality and importance of the bubble I lived in. I was able to reflect through the years and realize, for the most part, who I was and why. Understanding where we come from is monumental when it comes to developing relationships. Typically, we look for friends who come from similar backgrounds as we do. I still find it interesting that my best friends in college had very similar family structures and backgrounds as I did, but we didn't know it until after years of building friendship. Today, we have all structured our own families in nearly the same way. In fact, three of the four of us have four kids!

> "The definition of normal doesn't change because people are different from one another.

Not everyone at FHU came from the same place. It seemed obvious some came from what we called a much more "sheltered" background. One of our greatest flaws as college students was identifying and labeling others. It was a game at times. When we saw others who were different than we were, clearly, they weren't normal. Looking back, I wonder if they looked at us and wondered the same or, perhaps, they were better than that. I've come to believe "normal" is what is familiar to us. Normal starts in your home. With this in mind, everyone is unique and normal in their own right. The definition of normal doesn't change because people are different from one another.

I can't say enough good about the life my parents provided for me as a child and adolescent. As a young boy, I was taught to value people, not things or money. Some might say this aspect of my upbringing may have been, in part, because we couldn't afford the finer things in life, but this was not the case. I was unaware of our financial situation because my parents were frugal and showered us with constant love and time.

I remember playing sports, bowling, swimming, going to the skating rink, and many other activities when I was younger. More than that, I recall the importance of having a spiritual focus within our house. My dad was a preacher. He woke up every morning and spent an hour in prayer and study before he started in on his responsibilities with the church and sermon preparation. He has always been a diligent student, an excellent father, and example of a husband of which most women dream. My mom is the very definition of selflessness. I don't know if I'll ever understand the extent of what she did without, so we always had more than enough. When we were in school, she worked, and she saved so our "normal" was enjoyable. They may not realize it, but one of the greatest lessons I learned from my parents is this: normal is different for everyone. Don't compare your normal to someone else, just enjoy being normal for you. In doing so, stress will be minimized in your daily activities.

My parents gave me an example of contentment and selflessness for which I will forever be grateful. Now, as a father of four, I am even more thankful for their example. The need I have to give the same example to my kids is even more prevalent than ever. Benjamin Franklin said, "Contentment is what makes poor men rich. Discontentment makes rich men poor." Showing our kids how to be content early in life will be a great service to them down the road.

If you step out of your body for a minute and evaluate your life from the outside looking in, what do you see? What have you surrounded yourself with? Your job? Your friends? Your hobbies? Your car? Your house? Your faith? Your toys? Your spouse? Your kids?

We all have a freewill that allows us to choose many of our immediate surroundings. Some of us are fortunate enough to see and understand the gravity and weight of the decisions we make when we are young. Realizing there are consequences for our actions early in life is one of the greatest nuggets of wisdom that will make living without anxiety a more attainable option as we age. Any knowledge gained about appropriate decision making is an invaluable asset to everyone who lives with minimal stress.

Is it possible to live without worry and anxiety? In the first century, a man named Jesus said we should not worry about the clothes we wear or the food we eat because God provides for the birds of the air and the lilies of the field. He goes on to say we are much more valuable than they are. As we have already seen, the inspired writer Paul says in his letter to the church at Philippi, "Be anxious for nothing". One thing is very clear: Anxiety is a choice. How we respond to the consequences of the stress in our lives determines the anxiety we experience.

Whether you believe we are created by God or come into existence by other means, we exist with freewill. This is one of the greatest blessings in life. The negative side of this reality is we don't always use our freewill in the way we should. We are so moldable because of misconceptions of two very destructive ideas: Comparative living and normalcy.

Comparative Living

Comparative living is something everyone is affected by except the "Jones" family. They appear to be the standard by which everyone compares themselves. To whom do the Jones' family compare themselves? We all have people in our lives we want to be like. They might be our family, friends, enemies or even people we have never met. Our culture has created a standard and conditioned us to believe we must be like anyone but ourselves. Every form of media is used to remind us constantly of who is following what trend and which trend to follow and how to follow. It doesn't take long before someone else is telling us what to wear, what to drive, where to live, how many kids to have and how many people we should marry! This sounds like such a sad existence, doesn't it? Unfortunately, this is our reality. It is increasingly difficult to find contentment if we are constantly reminded of our need to compare ourselves to others.

Normalcy

Normalcy is another dangerous and destructive path that many of us don't understand. As an adjective, normal is defined as "conforming to a standard, usual, typical or expected" (www.dictionary.com). As a noun, it is defined as "the usual, average, or typical state or condition" (www.dictionary.com). With that in mind, how does this affect the stress we face every day? For most people, being normal is the goal. No one wants to hear he or she isn't normal. Because we want to be like everyone else, we are waiting to see the latest trend so that we know what we should do, even if the new "normal" doesn't make sense. How ironic is it that we ask our kids, "If everyone jumped off a cliff, would you?" Yet, here we are standing in line to jump off the cliff.

Here is some food for thought: The Bible never mentions the word "normal." We are not supposed to be "normal" or like everyone else. In fact, we are not supposed to be like everyone else at all. We are supposed to be like Jesus. He was a man so different from everyone else. While it may be more difficult to be like Jesus than everyone else, the reward is worth the challenge. In 1 Corinthians 11:1, Paul tells us to imitate him as he imitates Christ. He also says in Romans 12:2, *"Do not be conformed to this world but be transformed by the renewing of your mind."* Are we willing to accept this challenge or are we content accepting the challenge of being like the multitudes surrounding us? Are you normal?

My mother-in-law loves Christmas as much as anyone I know. She also owns more Christmas decorations than anyone I have ever met. Every year, around the beginning of October, she takes out the trees, lights, nativities, etc. Her attic and garage are filled with boxes of decorations and trees that could fill a hotel! She spends between four and six weeks putting out a wonderland in her house so that when people come to visit, they leave her house with the spirit of Christmas. It is a beautiful phenomenon. Does this sound normal to you?

If you have tons of Christmas decorations and spend three to four months focusing on the beauty of Christmas inside and outside your home, then yes, I imagine this sounds normal. I am not one of those people, not even close. This violates every fiber of my "normal." Our family loves Christmas, but we are conservative with the amount of time we spend decorating and the number of decorations we own. In fact, we spend about two hours on Thanksgiving Day putting ALL our decorations out. This is our tradition. We also spend about two hours taking it all down on Christmas evening. This is normal for us. I would like to think this is closer to "normal" for most folks. However, the truth is, normal means something different to everyone, and a spectrum spans so many styles and quantities it would be impossible to label any one group as normal.

What if I told you some people believe Jesus was born in June? What if there were some people who celebrated Christmas six months early or late? Would this really bother us? Would we think these people aren't "normal"? Why? We don't have proof of the exact date of the birth of Jesus. Truth be told, we weren't there. This is just one of many examples we could look at when determining what makes us or someone else normal.

Normal is different in every aspect of our lives. We may have a lot in common with the majority when it comes to the amount of time we spend watching TV or how we discipline our kids but completely different from the same large group of people when it comes to the kind of person we married, if and where we attend church and our political party affiliation.

What influences determine our circumstances?

I would suggest comparative living has more to do with the choices we make than anything else. For example, what determines the car we drive, the house we live in, and the toys we buy? What aids us in deciding whom we marry and the number of children we want in our home? What do we eat and how much do we exercise? We choose these things, but there are many external factors that assist us in our decision-making process. What and whom we expose ourselves to reveals a lot about what helps us understand our needs and our wants. It's been several years since we decided not to have cable television. We realized the powerful influences of commercialism and decided to do our best not to allow our little ones to be influenced by media. My kids, for the most part, are content with what they have until they see an advertisement for the newest toy at the store, and then, their "needs" change. We try to eliminate ads.

My wife Kristen and I recently sat down with our kids and asked them to identify our needs. I shouldn't have been as shocked as I was when our 8-year old daughter said, "food, clothing and shelter." Did I teach her that? I honestly couldn't remember teaching her those exact words, but I'm hoping it is something she has learned from the way we live. I imagine if we asked kids from several diverse backgrounds and families to write down a list of their needs and wants, we would get very different answers. As an adult, if you were to sit down and write out a list of your needs and wants, what would your lists look like?

I was taught from an early age to be happy with what I have. The very definition of contentment is just that; being happy with what you have. We didn't have a lot growing up, but we valued what we had. We will discuss more about materialism and contentment in the chapter on finances. It is important for us to realize the connection between contentment and stress. Stressful people are not usually happy people and happy people are not usually stressed out. It's hard to be both at the same time.

We live in a culture that tries to destroy any attempt we make at being content. As we raise our kids, we often think, "When will enough be enough?" The best definition I have heard of "enough" came from a finance class I was attending at our church. The definition given was "just a little bit more." I began to wonder if this was accurate in my own life? When will I have enough money? How much is enough food? How much is enough affection? How much is enough communication? How much is enough religion? What is enough at work? When will I have enough stuff?

Commercials are filled with antics to convince us of what we "need," not what we "want." In doing so, they take control of our minds to a certain extent. Sadly, we allow them to do this. How? Along with watching the commercial, we convince ourselves they know what we NEED in our life! When we consider our needs and wants, we should refer to what my 8-year old daughter told us a few nights ago: Food. Clothing. Shelter. We understand what we eat, our clothing preference, and what kind of house we live in are determined by several factors. However, if we take a realistic look at our budget and understand our lives are about more than filet mignon, name brands, and mansions, we will be more successful in eliminating a few of the stresses that so many struggle with on a daily basis.

In the entry way of our house, we placed a piece of art with the words of Philippians 4:12. It says, *"In any and all circumstances, I have learned the secret of being content."* This is the mantra or affirmation for our family. We see it every day when we leave the house and when we come home. It serves us as a constant reminder of knowing we can be happy with what we have. It's a choice we make. It also puts a good thought in the minds of guests when they come in our home as well.

Without a doubt, there is a connection between contentment and anxiety. The connection is this: they are opposites. We cannot live with both. We must choose to live a life of contentment or we are CHOOSING to live a life with anxiety. In our house, we choose contentment. My prayer and hope are to help you understand two things. You have the power to choose contentment. You have the power not to choose anxiety. These may sound like the same thing because they are; often, we need a different perspective to help us realize our choices.

I managed a business for several years before taking my current job, and I had the opportunity to work with and hire young adults. At every opportunity, I tried to give them advice that would help them be successful in life. I broke life down into three important decisions we must make:

1. Live like Jesus Christ. Whether you believe in God or not, our world will be a much better place when we all put the needs of others above our own. Jesus gave the world an unmatched example of perfection in the way to live life on this earth. If success is what you are after, practicing humility and selflessness toward people is the first step. We will discuss this in depth in the chapter on faithfulness.

23

2. Marry well. I have been blessed with opportunities to speak at churches, seminars, and conferences in the U.S. and several other countries in South and Central America. I have included these keys to success in some of my lessons when they fit the topic assigned. Often, when I say, "marry well," people hear "marry wealth." You can imagine the looks I get when the audience perceives I am promoting the need to marry for money. My definition of "well" is straight forward: Marry someone who loves God more than you. If you want to have success in life, success in your marriage is vital. When our spouse makes us second in their life because God is number one, only then can we understand the blessing of marriage God created for us. We will talk more about this in the marriage and stress chapter.

3. Acquire a job you love so much that if you didn't need money, you would still work the same job. A nominal factor in successful living is seen in how we work. Because most of us spend a considerable amount of time at our job each week, if we don't love what we do, it is going to be increasingly difficult to have a positive outlook when we come home from work. However, if we love what we do for a living, we will have a positive outlook when we leave for work and when we come home. We will talk more about this in the work and stress chapter.

We all have the power to make choices in these three areas of life. We choose how we treat others. We choose whom we marry. We choose where we work. People who live with little or no anxiety are the result of the culmination of good choices they have made in these areas. Later chapters discuss how the overflow in these three areas affects all the stressors in our life in some way.

In the last few years, my wife and I decided to minimize nearly all the stuff in our life. We haven't ever done much in the way of excess, but there is always room for improvement. After reading several books on minimalism, we reaffirmed our desire to focus on experiences and not possessions.

> *"A calm and humble life will bring more happiness than the pursuit of success and the constant restlessness that comes with it." – Albert Einstein*

Recently in the news, a napkin with a note written on it was sold for $1.3 million. Can you imagine? In 1922, after learning he would be awarded the Nobel Prize in physics, Albert Einstein needed to leave a tip for a bellboy, but he didn't have any money. He wrote a few words in German on the napkin and gave it to the bellboy and told him it would probably be worth more than a small tip. The note read:

"A calm and humble life will bring more happiness than the pursuit of success and the constant restlessness that comes with it."

Some advice is priceless. Apparently, you can put a price on advice from Albert Einstein, at least if you have the original copy. Something is to be said for the attitude of such a brilliant man. If we choose to remain calm and humble while focusing on the simplicity of creating a realistic life full of contentment and joy, surprises and circumstances we don't have control over will not rock our boat nearly as much. If we choose chaos and restlessness in the pursuit of worldly success, when things we can't control appear in our life, we will find ourselves on a boat that is very difficult to navigate.

As we determine our life choices, we should look at the word "necessity." In Philippians 4:19, Paul says *"I know my God will supply all of your needs according to His riches in glory by Christ Jesus."* We must understand the difference between our needs and wants. If something is needed, it can add a tremendous amount of value. We should focus on our needs and how we can use what we already have to live humbly. If we have an abundance of things we don't need, we should evaluate the amount of stress they cause and determine if they still have enough value to be in our life.

Our attitude toward our circumstances determines a great deal of the joy we experience in life. While many things are within our control, some big factors are outside our control. This is quite troublesome for those of us who wear the title "control freak." When we crave control, life becomes an internal (and sometimes external) quarrel as circumstances are thrust upon us and we can do nothing to change them. However, we can control much more than we think we can. It is easy to say, "That's out of my control" so we don't have to fix or change an attitude or behavior towards someone or something. Self-reflection can help us understand what is within our control.

The purpose of this book is not to convince you you're to blame for the stress and anxiety in your life, but rather to persuade you to look at the power within your being to create the change you want and need to see. Take a deep breath. Focus. Ask yourself if using T.R.I.A.L.S. can help you. For the next few chapters, I want to challenge you to really think about the application of the T.R.I.A.L.S. method and how it can help reduce the stress in your life.

Motivation: Each day, make a commitment to pray to God and tell Him you are willing to work on the area of life that causes you anxiety. He doesn't want you to live with it! Let's choose to be open about the anxiety we have and talk to God about it. Let's eliminate the word "normal" from our vocabulary!

Advice: Read the next nine chapters with an open mind. If you read something that benefits you, please share it with others.

Prayer: "Lord, I have believed lies from the enemy. Set me free from the lies and beliefs of worthlessness. Forgive me for clinging to the affirmations of others. Strengthen me to let go of this destructiveness by renewing my mind and heart. Let your Spirit guide me and teach me the way to go and help me see me as You do. Amen" (Turner, K)

Chapter 3 – Marriage and Anxiety

Before we married, my bride and I were obligated to go through one set of marriage counseling and the pleasure of going through another. The obligatory sessions we drudged through were the result of wanting to have our wedding in the church building belonging to a group that required their pastor to administer pre-marital counseling to anyone who was married in their location. This was the most minuscule of the requirements that still holds interesting memories for us. As you can imagine, it is difficult to get advice on marriage from someone who doesn't know you. I still don't remember much from the counseling sessions with the first pastor. However, I do remember the first session ended in a prayer that nearly impaired my hearing. I still laugh when I think about it. He asked us several questions to try to get to know us and it was awkward because of the mandatory nature of the meeting. At the end of the hour-long session, he asked us if he could pray with us (like he needed to ask our permission). I can remember, like it was yesterday, bowing my head and waiting for him to address God in prayer. The words "Holy Father" will forever be imprinted in my mind and my ear drum because he said them so loud I am certain folks in Canada began to bow their heads and wait for the "amen." Trying not to laugh during the remainder of the prayer was more challenging than it should have been. After getting in the car to head to lunch, Kristen and I both laughed for a while. It was one of the funniest moments we had together before we were married.

The second pre-marital counseling experience was much more practical and helpful to us. We were fortunate to have my dad officiate the wedding and one of his requirements, even though I was his son, was for us to attend his counseling sessions. Many of the questions and exercises he had us work through were aimed at helping us think about key areas of life most couples may not talk about prior to marriage. For example, we hadn't discussed how many kids we wanted. After one of our sessions, we realized we wanted two or three kids, depending, I suppose, on how the first two turned out. It is a good thing we discussed this because eleven years later we have four kids and wouldn't mind having a fifth if it were possible. However, the greatest piece of advice he gave us related to the three keys of a successful marriage: communication, communication, communication. You will continue to see this tool mentioned in this chapter and the rest of the chapters in this book.

Every journey we venture on will experience change. Without fail, events will happen and cause us to change our thoughts, movements, careers, actions, words, belief system, etc. Our reaction to these changes and how we use communication as we navigate through life will regulate our stress and anxiety levels. This is especially true in marriage.

I have been abundantly blessed when it comes to not having anxiety in my marriage. I don't have to hope my bride feels this way. I'm confident she does because we talk about it. We haven't arrived at a great marriage on accident. It has taken and continues to require great effort on our part to follow the teaching we see in scripture to treat each other the way God desires. The Bible teaches specific roles for men and women within the marriage relationship. In Ephesians 5, we read husbands are to love their wives as Christ loved the church. It then says, *"Wives submit to your husbands as to the Lord."*

This could be a very short chapter if we would all just read and apply what we find in Ephesians 5. However, there is certainly more to grab from this text and the experiences we have had within our marriage. One of my "takeaways" from this text is God places much more responsibility on the man within marriage than He does the woman. As Christ did more for the church than the church can ever do for Christ, men have a responsibility to do more for their bride than the bride can do for him. If husbands would love their wives as Christ loved the church, it would certainly make it easier for brides to submit to their husbands as to the Lord.

If we back up in the text, we see both sides have a responsibility to submit to each other. I have visited with people who have told me they can't love or submit to the opposite sex. One friend has told me she could never submit to a man. When I asked her if she would change her mind if she found a man to love her as Christ loved the church, she at least hesitated. It is sad some people have never seen an example of a marriage the way God designed.

I mentioned the three keys to successful living: Be a Christian, marry well, and have a job you love. What does it mean to marry well?   Is it possible to have a perfect marriage? Before you say "no," let's agree our answer to this question will depend on our definition of the word "perfect." When we see the word "perfect" in scripture, the definition is often translated as "complete or mature."   A perfect marriage is not something we wake up to one morning but rather we grow into.

While I have been married for only eleven years, and I would not consider myself an expert at anything, I do believe when common sense, preparation, and communication come together, they breed a recipe for the beauty we all desire to have within our marriages. It will also go a long way in helping us eliminate anxiety with the people we love the most in this life.

Common Sense

Merriam-Webster defines common sense as "sound and prudent judgment based on a simple perception of the situation or facts" (https://www.merriam-webster.com/). Because we live in a world of subjectivity, it is difficult to define words like sound and prudent. If we have a standard we adhere to, it becomes more evident what is common. For example, adding whole numbers is an exact science. Two plus two always equal four. This is an unchangeable fact. When ideas are introduced such as three plus one equals dog, we begin to see how foreign the idea of common sense seems to those who choose not to live by it. As crazy as this equation appears, it is not that far from the reality some schools are teaching our children about marriage and the home!

Personality traits, upbringing, life experiences, and many genetic predispositions also play a role in determining what is common within a marriage. One person may grow up in a Christian home, raised by God-fearing individuals who instilled the need and the desire to treat others by the golden rule, "Do unto others as you would have them do unto you." This is perhaps one of the most common rules for a Christian's life. What a wonderful world it would be if everyone abided by this principle!

Unfortunately, many, many others are born into families with physical, mental, and emotional abuse. Couple any of these with adults in a home that struggle with substance abuse, and you have a completely different view on what is common. While it is not impossible to escape these circumstances and have a successful life, it is exponentially more difficult than it is for those who are born into homes without these problems. It is also disheartening how many people I know who came from a God-fearing household and destroyed their own marriage because they lacked the sense and guidance needed to create harmony within their home.

What is common for one person may not be common to another. When this happens, it is helpful to explore the good, better, best options. At times opposites attract, and physical, emotional and spiritual chemistry is undeniable. At other times opposites do not attract, and people should flee from each other to save themselves. How do we know when to stay and when to run? How do we know when to explore potential?

When teenagers and even preteens begin to explore relationships outside of friendship, all the aforementioned descriptors play a role in how feelings are developed. I can remember wanting to date girls when I was in junior high and high school. It seemed like all the "good girls" wanted to date the "bad guys." I was labeled many things as a teenager, but "bad" was not one of them. I did my best to treat other people, especially ladies, with respect and kindness. Why was it so difficult to find a girlfriend? I came from a good family. I treated other people well. I had good friends. I don't think I was horribly unattractive. I played sports and did well in school. I was doing everything right and still couldn't find a girlfriend. Was there something wrong with me I wasn't seeing? Could everyone else see I wasn't ready for that kind of relationship but me?

To say the least, this is a lot of stress for a teenager to handle. Fortunately, having a girlfriend was not the priority of my young life. While it would have been considered a bonus by my own standards, it wasn't necessary at that point in time. I was able to learn at an early age the importance of learning. Understanding relationships and responsibilities became vital in my development as a person. I can confidently say I was a "late bloomer" in many regards. Most would have seen this as a negative, but I believe it was one of the greatest blessings to me then and especially now. What became common to me was having patience in developing myself. Having a good understanding of who I was as a person enabled me to learn who I needed to become. It also provided me intuition regarding what to expect of myself before I placed expectations on someone else, especially a potential spouse.

This ability and maturity are rarely seen in teenagers, which is why we need to encourage young people to learn who they are before they try to learn about others. If we are successful in this endeavor, perhaps fewer people will avoid the mistake of making a lifelong commitment prematurely. If more and more people take this path, it will become common for people not to rush into marriage for the wrong reasons. Ultimately, patience in choosing our mate will provide us the tools we need to have less stress with our spouse, regardless of our age.

When it comes to what should be common within a marriage, the Bible should always be our guide. The Bible is clear in Ephesians 5 regarding what common looks like within the marriage relationship. Jesus is clear in Matthew 19 what the consequences are for those who commit to marriage and then decide it is not for them. We should heed His teaching.

On a very personal note, my advice on dating for any person, especially young people, is this: If you aren't ready to get married, there is no need for you to be in a dating relationship.

Preparation

This step is not only important before we get married, but equally important after we marry. Every single day we should wake up looking for ways to prepare ourselves to be

> *Every single day we should wake up looking for ways to prepare ourselves to be better in our marriage.*

better in our marriage. If we want to grow in our marriage, we have to constantly change. The goal is for our marriage to get better every day. This may require some creativity. This may require some patience. The blessing is worth the work.

For those of us already married, I imagine we know with certainty whether we were prepared when we began our marriage or not. It is probable many of us would say nothing can prepare someone for marriage but to that end, I disagree. If we truly believe nothing can prepare someone for marriage, there would be no point in trying. Who wants to make any effort at something knowing they will fail? Better yet, why would the next generation put forth any effort if our example teaches them it is impossible to be prepared for marriage? It is obvious the marital preparation phase of life in our culture needs much improvement.

When we talk about being prepared for marriage, usually a very large elephant is in the room. Sometimes, he is sneaky and doesn't get noticed for a while, but most of the time, this awkward monster sits in the middle of the room and tries to make us all feel uncomfortable. How uncomfortable do we get when we hear the word "sex" used in conversation? Does it depend on who is in the room? Are we comfortable around our peers talking about it, but uncomfortable around strangers, our spouse, our parents, our children, co-workers, or church members? While I want to address this topic as it relates to preparing our children for marriage, this is not the only area that needs preparation. Marriages consist of so much more than the "two become one flesh" physical aspect of the relationship.

To make sure the elephant has a comfortable seat, let's greet him first in this discussion. For men and women, the sexual aspect of a relationship creates different levels of stress. In many cases, the lack of sex creates more stress for men and less stress for women. When neither communicates their feelings about sex, this can become a much bigger problem.

I have never been bold enough to ask a group during a class or seminar for a show of hands for all those who had ever experienced intimacy problems. Who wants to admit they have intimacy issues? Since you are reading this book, you can answer this question for yourself. If you have intimacy problems, my suggestion is this: Make intimacy a priority in your marriage. How does this happen?

Be intimate with your spouse! Communicate! Even if it's awkward, communicate. Communicate.

Gary Chapman, author of _The Five Love Languages_, defines five ways love is communicated in relationships. One of the languages is physical touch and most men say this is their primary love language. Why does this become such a complicated issue within marriage? Do women punish men by withholding intimacy? If women were willing to be more intimate all the time, would every relationship thrive? The short answer is NO! Marriages are about more than intimacy. Intimacy does not just mean sex. Whatever issue(s) come up, communication is the way to solve them!

> _We should not expect something from a future spouse we are unwilling to expect of ourselves._

I am qualified to address only two groups of people on the topic of intimacy. The first group is those who have never been married. Many years ago, I was single and looking for someone to spend the rest of my life with. Whether you are single or looking for a relationship, your expectations regarding intimacy of a potential spouse are important to communicate. Keep in mind, we should not expect something from a future spouse we are unwilling to expect of ourselves. I have known people who were sexually active in high school and college who expected their potential spouse to be a virgin. How much sense does that make?

The time to have conversations about the expectations of intimacy before and after marriage may not be on the first date. However, if this aspect of a relationship is important to you and you have set expectations for yourself that you intend to expect from others, you shouldn't delay too long. If sex before marriage is a deal breaker for you, it's important to understand your potential spouse's past sooner rather than later. Before you determine your deal breakers, I'd also encourage you to read Matthew 18. It is interesting that Jesus teaches about forgiveness before He teaches about divorce.

The second group pertains to those who are married and enjoy intimacy within their marriage. One of the most difficult topics to teach about or even talk about is sex. Intimacy is about so much more than sex though. Intimacy is about being close to someone. If you follow my advice in the previous section about those who are not yet married, the intimacy within your marriage will benefit greatly. The key is communication.

Intimacy problems are a result of poor or no communication. If you are struggling in intimacy, talk to your spouse! Every time communication is the problem, it is also the solution. My wife and I have no secrets. We enjoy intimacy within our marriage because we talk about it and we make it a priority. You don't need a sermon on this topic to understand the benefits of intimacy in your marriage. I encourage you to read *The Five Love Languages* by Gary Chapman for more information about communication and love. It is a great book!

The dating relationship is a precursor for marriage. Personally, if the goal of a dating relationship isn't marriage, I don't see the point. For that reason, I don't plan to "allow" my kids to date before they are ready to think about marriage. This doesn't mean it is wrong to date when you are young. I dated a few girls before I met my wife, but I wasn't near ready for marriage. Many people date to experience how to treat a girl. Boys may want to get experience kissing (or more), meeting future in-laws, opening doors, etc. Girls may want to figure out if there are any gentleman left in the world. Sadly, these explorations seem to begin at a younger age every year and rarely end well.

The responsibility of helping prepare those who are unmarried belongs to those who are married. Guide them in the key areas of this book regarding stress: work, finance, marriage, parenting, health, and faith.

Communication

I am blessed to be married to a woman who believes in the importance and vitality of effective communication within marriage. I don't know if there is such a thing as a "perfect marriage," but my wife and I both agree ours is pretty close. I credit our great marriage to communication. We don't hold in and we don't hold back. If you have effective communication, there must be transparency and honesty, and at the same time, the delivery of this communication must be encompassed with love. There may be awkward moments, perhaps even uncomfortable, but a moment of discomfort is better than dealing with anxiety or an explosion of frustration, especially at an inopportune time. We have learned it is best to deal with any issues or disagreements that come up as soon as possible. Waiting to communicate causes one of two things: forgetting details or amplifying frustrations. Neither of these two results is desirable.

If you are not married, one of the greatest qualities you can find in your potential spouse is that of an effective communicator. If you must constantly guess what your loved one is thinking, you will find a life full of anxiety, fear and irritation. If you are married, it is my hope you and your spouse both communicate well with each other. If this is not the case, I encourage and challenge you to make a priority of changing this component in your relationship. It will do nothing but help in resolving any challenges you face together.

Some of the most important things to communicate to a spouse are the obvious. In the twelve years I have been married, I have learned the necessity and the blessings of telling my wife all the things she already knows. Just because she knows I love her doesn't mean I don't need to tell her. She knows she is the most beautiful woman in the world to me, but that doesn't mean I shouldn't continue telling her. I don't have to guess if she thinks I am attractive because she tells me. It's hard not to have a smile on your face and feel good about yourself when your spouse is telling you how strong, smart, attractive or talented you are! Building up your spouse and being specific is a very important aspect of communication. I've heard it said, "Tell your wife she is what you want her to be and that's what she will become. Tell her she is a number of negative things and that's what she will become."

Excellent communication does not happen by accident. Several years ago, I gave my bride a gift for Christmas that took a tremendous amount of time to create. I made 52 gift certificates with a promise to have coffee every Sunday afternoon while she opened one of them for a year. I designed each certificate intentionally and put each one in a separate envelope. I also paid someone to write the week and number on every envelope in calligraphy. Without a doubt, this was the best gift I had ever given her. It wasn't what was written on the certificates that she enjoyed the most, but the time we spent together every Sunday afternoon. Sure, some of the certificates didn't cost a lot to deliver on. For example, a 30-minute hand or foot massage didn't cost me more than the time and energy it took to rub her hands and feet. There were also some she enjoyed more than others like the "I'll do dishes for a week" and "I'll do laundry for a week." Again, while she enjoyed the contents of each certificate, it is the time we spent over coffee she loved the most.

The subsequent years, we realized this is a gift we should repeat. Designing and making 52 certificates every year would be quite an undertaking, but if you have the time, you won't regret giving the gift. For us, we realized how important quality time and communication are in our marriage. About two years ago, we determined we needed and wanted more than just Sunday afternoon together, so we decided to have more. Now, nearly every day, we sit down at some time between noon and 2:00 PM, and we have coffee or tea and discuss our life, our kids, and our day. Sometimes I may be travelling when this doesn't happen, but if I am home, we never miss this opportunity. When aspects of our marriage are a priority and important, we will make whatever "sacrifices" are needed if we want to have less stress in our marriage. For us, it was making time to communicate without distractions. What will it be for you?

I know a lot of married people and very few of them would say they have a "perfect marriage" although I know some that would say they are close. Any time an additional member is added to a household, whether a spouse or children, stressors arise. Our reaction to these stressors determines the amount of anxiety we allow to enter our marriage. Understanding the differences between us and our fiancée is not just helpful but vital in helping us learn how stress management takes place when the two become one. I would also suggest understanding the differences between us and those we date is just as significant.

I don't know of a more bizarre system of pre-marriage relationships than what exists in our culture today. People seem so afraid of commitment; they have invented as many ways as possible to test boundaries and push limits while remaining a "couple" without saying "I do." We live in a time when the younger generations so desperately need to see successful, committed marriages, but it isn't going to happen by accident. Perhaps if we didn't train ourselves and our kids to obtain the kind of relationships we see in Hollywood; we would see more success and less anxiety in marriage. Perhaps if we took more time to get to know a potential spouse through communication instead of physical attraction, money, status, etc., we would see a significant increase in successful marriages.

Once we tie the knot and finally come to the realization that boys are different from girls, how do we live in unity and harmony with the one to whom we have committed the rest of our lives? Before we look at T.R.I.A.L.S. to help reduce stress before and after marriage, we need to have a proper understanding of goals and expectations.

Goals and expectations in marriage:

Our goals and expectations are going to be different. Like most areas in our marriage, our goal is perfection. Our expectation is to give our best effort. If we put this into practice, we will find it easier to forgive when we or our spouse miss the mark. Remember, we want to be perfect and we are making our best effort. Let's give each other a little grace when we fall short. A positive and forgiving attitude will help us decrease stress as we create a healthy environment in our home.

Not one of us is ever going to be perfect in the sense we won't make mistakes. It isn't possible. This doesn't mean we don't aim for it. If we aim for perfection and give all we can, we have no reason for regret, stress or anxiety.

Think about the piece of advice you would give to others to improve their marriage. What is the greatest lesson you have learned within your marriage? If there are things you find beneficial in your marriage, share them with those who are asking for advice or help. If I could offer just one piece of advice to you, it would be this: Don't compare your marriage to anyone else's marriage. Comparative living is never helpful in any aspect of life, especially marriage. Be the best version of yourself and serve your spouse.

If stress or anxiety begins to show up in your marriage, slow down and look at how T.R.I.A.L.S. can help you maintain peace with your spouse.

Transparency – Honesty and trust. Even if it's awkward and uncomfortable, we must learn to communicate the truth, the whole truth and nothing but the truth to our spouse. Communication is important in every part of T.R.I.A.L.S., but it is the most important when it comes to transparency. Nothing will tear two people apart like lies, secrets, and distrust. Transparency does more than prevent negativity in marriage; it also promotes positivity. When there are no secrets or distrust, the open air between two people is more than refreshing! Enjoy the spouse of your youth!

Responsibility – Owning your past and preparing for the future. We have all done things we are not proud of in the past. All. Of. Us. When we talk about delicate topics with our spouse, we must be respectful and kind as we admit our previous faults. We must also be understanding when our spouse is admitting their faults. More importantly, we must learn from our past to help prepare for the future and help our kids not make the same mistakes we made. If we want a great marriage, it will require careful planning and communication about jobs, finances, parenting, health, and faith.

Intentionality – Great marriages do not happen by accident. It takes hard work, communication, and sacrifice. All of these must be done with intention and purpose. Far too often, we do things without thinking and giving purpose to our actions. We react harshly to words that hurt us, even if the intention was not to hurt us. This usually leads to conflict. If we pause before making decisions or if we spend some time at the beginning of each day deciding what our plan will be, our decision making is much easier. If we wake up each morning and decide the wrong or unethical choice is not an option, making the right choice is always easier. Within the context of marriage, it is vital for us to be intentional with the way we treat our spouse, with our words and our actions.

Appreciation – Two of the most under-used words are "Thank you." When our roles become common or expected, expressing gratitude can become a thing of the past. We cannot let this happen. The expectations of husbands and wives in the home is different in each culture. Regardless of our culture, we must continue to show gratitude. If you follow the T.R.I.A.L.S. method, it is extremely important to be grateful when your spouse is transparent, responsible and intentional. This is not easy. You must be vulnerable and open to suggestion. Find ways to express your gratitude that show your spouse love. I've mentioned *The Five Love Languages* as a good resource for understanding how to communicate love to your spouse. If you don't know how your spouse wants to be appreciated, ask her or him. Playing the guessing game rarely works out for either side in this equation.

Limits – Everyone has a limit or a breaking point. Our buttons can be pushed only so many times. Tolerance is an important word to understand when it comes to limits in marriage. There are positive and negative limits. We can be overwhelmed when someone is pushing us to our limits of patience in an argument or discussion about difficult topics. We can also become overwhelmed when someone is doing too much for us. If we are uncertain what our limits are, we need to learn them. Naturally, when we are getting closer to our limits, and situations are escalating, whether good or bad, we need to slow down. A good habit or rule to have is a safe word. Once you understand your limits, when you feel you are getting too close to them, have a word you can use with your spouse that calms the situation. Don't push limits.

We never want to be at a boiling point and say or do things we will regret.

Simplify – Married life can be so busy. When we are asked, "How are you doing?" how often do we respond "busy"? We fill every second with something to do or somewhere to go and it becomes difficult to slow down and enjoy any moments. When we find ourselves constantly on the run, communication often finds itself overlooked and in the backseat. Anxiety and stress begin to creep in because of the pressure we put on ourselves to stay busy. We need to learn the value of simplifying. In our marriage, we should ask ourselves, "Would life be less stressful if we didn't _____ this week, tomorrow, today?" When it comes to responsibilities we put on our plate that take time away from our spouse, can we delegate some of these to someone who has less on their plate to take care of them? What if we learn to say "no"?

If you are the kind of people that get asked to serve others all the time, you understand the great blessing of being involved in service. However, there are times when we must politely decline so that we can make sure we have enough time for our spouse. Decline, delegate and evaluate. Simplify.

Motivation: To the married: Take time to have an open conversation with your spouse this week. Be transparent. LAUGH. Express love. Ask for one thing you can do to show your spouse you love and appreciate them. Next week, repeat. The week after that, I hope you get it by now.

To the unmarried who have been married before: Find a way to encourage people who are married or looking to get married. Share knowledge you have gained from having been married.

To those looking to marry: Be patient. Pray. Become the perfect spouse before you expect the perfect spouse.

Pray. Put God first and look for a potential spouse who does this also.

Advice: Be a good listener. Don't aim for average or "normal." Love God first, then your spouse. If you do this correctly, your spouse will be blessed because of it.

Prayer: Thank you for life. Thank you for freewill and freedom. Help me to be a good communicator. Help me to be a good listener. Help me to help and teach those younger than me the importance of preparation and communication before they marry, that they may have a proper perspective of how you designed the marriage relationship. May you be glorified in all my relationships. Amen.

Chapter 4 – Parenting and Anxiety

There are many days that change a person's life forever. I'm not sure if any day has been more monumental for my wife and me than the birth of our first child. It wasn't just the day of birth that brought us overwhelming joy, but the process of learning the gender, selecting a name, baby showers, hospital stays, and first doctor appointments are just a few of the experiences imprinted in our minds. We smiled and cried through it all.

Now, as parents of four, one of our goals is to live in such a way that when our daughters are ready to look for a husband, they want to find a man who will treat them the way I treat their mother. For our sons, we want them to look for a wife who will treat them the way their mother treats me. If we cannot say this is the goal, we need to re-evaluate the example we are putting in front of our kids.

Of all the areas in life, parenting gives me the most stress. This is mainly stress I put on myself to raise them in a certain way. Many situations and variables are presented to us daily and stress comes from everywhere. However, all these stressors do not force me to have anxiety. They certainly provide opportunity for anxiety, but the choice is still mine. I still choose peace. I still choose not to be overwhelmed. I still choose.

Before we had children, I remember having friends who were already parents and the joy I had of looking forward to having some of our own. I don't recall thinking parenting would be easy. However, there were some situations where we had been better prepared. I don't know if anyone could have said something to prepare us adequately for parenthood.

I remember so well how naive I was before our children were born. I was not nearly as smart as I thought I was, and my children are constantly teaching me that lesson. For example, I thought there were only two possible personalities my wife and I would be able to produce among our children. They would each be like her or like me. I like my wife and I like me, so everything looked pretty good. What other options are there? We originally planned to have two or three children and decided later to have a fourth. I don't know if there could be four personalities more unique and different from one another than those of our kids.

I have on occasion taken all four of the kids to the grocery store when we needed to get a few items and my bride wasn't at home or able to go with us. I have a college roommate who also has four kids. We talk from time to time about the looks we get when people see us with four kids while mom is somewhere else. It is rarely a look of joy and congratulations! It is usually a "what were you thinking?" or "why didn't you stop?" kind of look. I choose to ignore the negative and embrace the positive.

I'm often asked if it is difficult to have four kids instead of one or maybe two. The answer for our family is yes and no. Having one child is a big change for parents because attention now has to be shared. Having a second child is often a bigger change for the first child because he or she must learn to share attention. Without a doubt, adding a third child was the greatest challenge for us. It is not because our third child was difficult, but when you are outnumbered, life is always more challenging. Adding a fourth child was not difficult at all for us. Our oldest had just turned 8 a few months before our youngest was born and she has been more of a help than anything. I am grateful for the blessings my kids have all brought to my life but especially the sense of community and help we provide for each other.

Life as a parent is not all rainbows and butterflies. As much as I would like to tell you raising kids will never add stress to your life, it is simply not true. If you think back to chapter two, we mentioned in the beginning of this book, kids are something we choose to put in our life. Most of us can control that input. However, we cannot control the way our kids always act. Because of the nature of free will, children can add a tremendous amount of stress to our life, especially if we do nothing to prepare them and ourselves for the challenges that some relationships bring.

My wife and I have read more parenting books than I knew existed a few years ago. She has read many more than I. I don't know if I would recommend one book more than another because every kid is different. Some books teach the need not to punish

> *When we find something that works, we should stick with it. That's wisdom.*

children physically but to only use words to build up and instruct. Other books speak to the need of each child having physical punishment to learn from mistakes. There are so many questions we ask as we incorporate various methods of parenting. How long should we try each method? Should we combine methods? Does it matter which method we use? Are we going to fail regardless of what we try with some of our kids and have success with others?

At the end of the day, we need to find a way to have peace with the decisions we make. Peace, not anxiety. I don't have all the answers to parenting. I don't believe any human being does. We should learn from our successes, failures, and experiences. Perhaps the most difficult advice to accept is that wisdom comes from experience. Some good, some bad. One of the keys to raising good kids is consistency. When we find something that works, we should stick with it. That's wisdom. I've learned the things that work best with my kids are not always easy at first. Tough love is tough sometimes.

The good news is it gets easier…sometimes. When it doesn't get easier, we must have the grit to stick with it regardless.

Some of us may have what we call a stubborn child or a "strong-willed" child. These children may require more effort from us as parents. Prior to a year ago, when our oldest son was four, I came close to the end of my rope with him. The only time we spanked him was when he hit one of his siblings, which was not very often. Much of the research we had done helped us understand the best ways for us to handle some aspects of his strong will. I will (likely) always remember the time I spanked him after he had hit one of his sisters. After I spanked him, we squared off so I could hug him and tell him I loved him. Before we came in for that embrace, he punched me square in the jaw, like a man. I was stunned to say the least. He then received another spanking which he may never forget. At least he hasn't punched me since then. He can be so stubborn at times!

We realized his stubbornness at an early age, and for a few years I tried to do something I realized later was ineffective for me. I tried to change him. I tried to change his strong will. Thankfully, I realized we cannot change the personalities of our children. We can help guide them on the path of righteousness and try to adjust their attitude when needed, but we cannot change their personality. I had to ask myself a few questions. Who am I to change a person God created? What if God created this young man with a strong will so that he can be a great leader one day? Who am I to stifle that just because he doesn't do everything the way I think he should? Shame on me for not realizing sooner what a blessing it was to have the privilege of raising a strong young man, even if it is difficult at times. I've since repented and decided to do what I can to provide him the tools he needs to harness his creativity and continue to become who God created.

> *Never take away love as a form of punishment.*

Gary Chapman is the author of _The 5 Love Languages._ It is a great book for all people to read, and especially people considering marriage. We recently discovered he authored another book,_ The 5 Love Languages for Kids_. One of the points he makes about parenting is that we should never take away love as a form of punishment. As I read the words, I got a lump in my throat. I realized how intentional I had been at times to punish my kids by taking something away from them they enjoyed. It's all a learning process. All kids need our time, and a lot of it. Some thrive on our time and need more than others. If our options are to take away a toy or to withhold our time as a form of punishment, it is a good idea to get rid of the toy. You can get more toys, but you can't get more time. We all need to figure out what our child's primary love language is and work to build him or her up by expressing love in the form they prefer to receive it. When it is necessary to punish, we must figure out what works best and be consistent.

From the time kids can understand and speak, communication becomes the most essential part of life. Children can communicate from a very early age, but it may not always be intelligible. We spend so much time as young parents trying to figure out what the child wants to communicate. We can usually tell when the child is telling us they need to have a diaper changed or they need to go to the bathroom. When they are hungry, a scream usually lets us know they need to eat. You have likely heard of a man named Maslow but if you haven't, I encourage you to look at his chart and the needs of children as they age. It may change the way you respond to the needs of your children.

There are also times when kids try to communicate but cannot because they don't know how to use words yet. When our second child was eighteen months old, she screamed. A lot. She had all her regular checkups with doctors. We didn't miss any appointments, but we could not figure out the behavioral issues we experienced. Finally, after listening to several suggestions, someone suggested we get her hearing tested. At the same time, we decided to get her eyes checked because it seemed like she might have an eye issue. After a few appointments, we realized she had not been able to hear for quite some time. We also learned she could hardly see anything. The lenses she was prescribed were as thick as any lenses I had ever seen. Can you imagine the life differences it made for an infant who was finally able to see and hear for the first time? She was like a new person!

Think about the role communication plays in all of this. Our little girl didn't respond to us when we talked to her because she was unable to hear. She was a little off balanced and not very coordinated because she couldn't see. Several years later, she is one of the most energetic, athletic little girls you will ever meet. If she has pain in her ears or eyes, she can understand the questions we ask and help us solve the problems that exist. In any relationship, especially parent to child, communication is vital.

After we get a proper view on the importance of communication between us and our children, we then must deal with understanding the definition of two key words when it comes to parenting: Discipline and Punishment. Discipline means to educate or instruct. Punishment is a consequence given for disobedience. Without fail, every child at some point needs to be punished. None of them are perfect. Some children need more punishment than others. All four of our children vary in the amount of punishment needed over the years. Discipline, however, is something that takes place daily in our house for all of us.

Our most important job as parents is to discipline or "educate and instruct" our children "in the Lord." Our reaction to our children when they make good choices is a form of discipline. Our reaction when they make bad choices is perhaps a more powerful form of discipline or at least one they will remember. Often, we become afraid of discipline because of several factors.

What scares you the most about being a parent?

Losing control

Having the answers

Raising entitled kids

Judgment

Someone getting hurt

Chaos

Not having all the answers

The struggle is different for all of us. When we find ourselves wanting to lash out at our kids, we need to take a deep breath and consider some alternatives to the negatively charged responses we sometimes give our precious little ones. For example, instead of threatening with "stop it or else _____," we could say, "I'm not sure what to do and that's ok." Admitting to our children we don't have it all figured out or we don't have all the answers is a great relationship building exercise. Learning together is better than being domineering or authoritative. Instead of complaining about how we have to do everything, we could reach out to our kids to ask them to help us. Admitting when we are angry and talking it out is better than exploding on our children. We need to learn we are capable of being in control all the time. If we will learn to handle stress appropriately, we can eliminate anxiety from being present in our lives.

As we begin to think about the trials we face as our children become teens and young adults, we must keep in mind relationships and start parenting as soon as children enter our house. Incorporating the T.R.I.A.L.S. method into parenting can be done whether the child is yours biologically or otherwise. Regardless of the way we raised or currently raise our kids, I challenge us all to incorporate the T.R.I.A.L.S. method into our daily routine with our kids.

Transparency – This is key in any relationship, but especially with kids. Am I withholding information from my children that would be beneficial in our relationship? Do I keep secrets from my children? If I learn things about my kids, do I feel comfortable with confrontation? The older kids get; the more transparency is needed. They don't need to live in doubt regarding how we feel about anything. The key to transparency is communication.

Sit down with your children this week. Plan a date or meeting or time you can sit and visit about life. Regardless of their age, if you have any questions you want/need to ask, be blunt and ask them, but do it with kindness. Ask your children if they have any worries, doubts or questions they want to talk to you about. Children need this kind of open relationship. If we want to reduce stress within our relationships with our kids, it starts with transparency and communication.

Responsibility – As in every aspect of our lives, we all make mistakes. Parenting is no exception. Taking responsibility for past mistakes is important in stress reduction. One of the ways we can do this is by talking about past mistakes and asking our kids for forgiveness. Make a plan to take responsibility moving forward. If you make a promise, keep it. Set reachable goals and talk to your kids about how you will reach them together. Communication and follow-up are crucial.

Intentionality – Good relationships with our kids don't happen by accident. Reading books, playing games, playing ball, etc. are intentional activities. Being intentional requires time and effort. It also requires us to be in the same place as our feet. Our kids notice when we are multi-tasking and only give them half of our attention, if that. If we want to create a healthy relationship with minimal stress between us and our kids, it will require much effort and intention. The work is worth the reward!

Appreciation – Showing appreciation towards our kids is a critical component of reducing stress in parenting. Our children must know how much we love and appreciate the good decisions they make. Appreciation is seen in our words and our actions. If we will look for creative ways to express our gratitude, stress is reduced, and we enjoy special moments with our precious little ones and adolescents. The most critical factor in showing appreciation is understanding how a child wants to be thanked. Being grateful is always beneficial, but we must learn to appreciate people in the way they want to be appreciated.

Limits – We all have limits. Our kids have limits. We should be very careful not to push ourselves or our kids to their limits. When conversations and situations get heated, it is wise to take a break and listen. When we reach our limits, emotions often get the best of us and we say things we don't mean and are unable to take back. This only escalates stress levels. Before things get out of hand, we must know our limits and avoid pushing them.

In our home, if kids are not behaving and we feel we are nearing our limits, we say "safe word." Whichever of us is in the driver's seat of disciplining our kids, the other is usually right there to keep the situation calm. We have some friends that told us they had a safe word they use when tempers escalate. We decided to say "safe word" because we couldn't come up with something more specific. Shockingly enough, it works!

Simplify – One of the greatest challenges of parenting is teaching our kids how to live a simple life. This is increasingly more difficult if we compare or our kids compare what we have to others. Part of simplifying is finding contentment. In fact, if we can find contentment in having less than what we have, simplifying becomes a much easier process. This is a learned process and our kids are learning from our example. Where and what we find contentment in is constantly being observed.

There are so many distractions. If extracurriculars, technology, or materialism is getting in the way of your relationship with your children, it is time to get rid of the distractions. It may be uncomfortable or irritating to your kids, but you need to be the greatest influence in their life. Spend more time with them than they spend with sports, TV, stuff, etc.

Motivation: Take time to sit down with your kids (regardless of their age) and talk openly about things you do well as a parent and ask them if there are areas they wished you would improve. BE HONEST! Embrace their perspective and work together as a family to be the best examples for each other possible.

I have to share what happened to us. When we did this with our kids, we learned a lesson on how we should show gratitude to them. All three of our kids said the area we could improve was spending more time with them. They didn't want more toys or food or anything else but our time. Listen to your kids when they tell you where you can improve.

Advice: If I could offer you one piece of advice when it comes to raising your kids, it would be this: Don't compare them to each other or to other people's kids. Comparing will never be helpful to anyone. This will be much easier if we eliminate the word "normal" from our life in all regards.

Prayer: Thank you for allowing me to be your child. Thank you for children. Help me to find the best ways to train them to be faithful Christians. If there are attitudes within me I need to change to help my kids, mold me into the person you desire of me. Make me a servant, Lord, make me like you. Amen.

Chapter 5 – Work and Anxiety

If you search online for the most stressful jobs, you are likely to find a list similar to the following:

Top 10 most stressful jobs:

1. Enlisted Military Personnel

2. Firefighter

3. Airline Pilot

4. Police Officer

5. Event coordinator

6. Public Relations Executive

7. Senior Corporate Executive

8. Broadcaster

9. News Reporter

10. Taxi Driver

This may not be the list you would have come up with, but this is the reality of the world wide web when it comes to stressful jobs. When I look at this list, I note the first four jobs mentioned all have some form of uncertainty when it comes to safety and so it makes sense for these jobs to be stressful. Jobs 5 – 9 on the list all have time demands, communication deadlines, and/or public speaking requirements. Given that most people are more afraid of public speaking than they are of dying, this also makes sense. How did taxi drivers make the list? I'm not sure, but they are stressed out.

What is our dream job? Is there such a thing? Did it make the list above? For some, a "dream job" may mean not working at all. For others, there is a more clear-cut answer, but it may be an unattainable job. What is it that drives us each day? Is it passion for going to a desk for 8-10 hours and waiting for Friday when we get our paycheck so that we can pay our bills, put food on the table, and, hopefully, have enough money for a date night? Is it the amount of money or the quality of life it provides? What is it about work that motivates us? If the answer is "I don't know" or "nothing about my job motivates me," perhaps we are stuck in a job of mediocrity and it is time for a change of job or a change of perspective.

Does our job add stress to our life? There are very few people who can confidently say their job brings no stress to their life. One of the three keys to successful living I mentioned in an earlier chapter is having a job you love so much if you didn't need any money, you would still work the same job. I can't imagine anyone would choose to go to a stressful job if they didn't need money. If we work primarily because we need money, it makes sense to choose a career path with as little stress as possible.

Considering the opportunities that exist in the U.S., nearly everyone has a choice about where to work. This may not apply to everyone, but it applies to most. If you are stuck in an overwhelmingly stressful job you don't like, it is time to consider making some changes. Remember, our jobs are one of the stressors we choose. If we choose a stressful job or the job we chose didn't start out as stressful but now gives us more anxiety than we can handle, we need to consider change within the work place or consider looking for a different workplace.

After graduating with a degree in Spanish, I went back to work for a swimming pool company I had worked for during my high school and college years. It was a safe choice and it made ends meet. There wasn't a great deal of stress involved in this job. However, it wasn't a job I loved. When the opportunity presented itself to put my degree to use, I took advantage as quickly as possible. I loved speaking Spanish and helping people. Like everyone, I also enjoyed job security. My new job was working in a call center for the "call before you dig" company. I was the only man working in the call center and I was also the only person who spoke Spanish. One of these circumstances made me feel very important and the other made my job a little less than enjoyable at times. I'll leave it up in the air as to which was which.

Not long after this career change, I was offered a promotion to do some voice over work and to continue translating for all the calls that needed a translator. I was also asked to teach a Spanish class to all the employees who were interested in learning Spanish which would also provide me with some additional income. Whether at church, work, or in the community, I love teaching any subject I am passionate and knowledgeable about. Two weeks before the first scheduled Spanish class I was going to teach, I had a meeting with my boss about the promotion I was to receive. Everything seemed perfect except what I believed to be the most important thing. At the end of the meeting, I asked what the salary cap would be for the new position. I wanted to know how much potential money I could make in a few years. The look on my face after they answered my question must have been easy to read. To say the least, I was not impressed, nor did I see my future in the company.

Fortunately, I had recently received a call from my previous employer asking if I would be interested in going back to work on salary. I was asked how much money I needed to come back to work. I took two days to think over the decisions I had in front of me. Both jobs had pros and cons but, in the end, I took the job that was going to pay the most, even if it meant I had to work nearly every Saturday of the year. The good news was I could pick any day off except Friday, Saturday or Monday. Let's see, that leaves Tuesday, Wednesday and Thursday. None of those days sounded like a good day off! This caused me to resent my job a little, and

I was the one that made the choice! I knew this would be the case long before I accepted the job, but my desire to make more money and my view of money trumped the inconveniences of my work schedule.

> If we can't change our career path, we must change the way we see our job.

What about you? What influences determine which job is ideal for you? Do you love your current job? Do you have options? Early in my career, I had options, but I didn't love either of them. I was working for a paycheck. Any time we don't like our job and we are working only for money, there will be stress. The key to overcoming stress in work-related situations is perspective. If we can't change our career path, we must change the way we see our job.

According to the American Psychology Association, there are many short-term and long-term side effects of work-related stress:

Short-Term:

headache, stomachache, sleep disturbances, short temper and difficulty concentrating.

Long-Term or Chronic Stress:

anxiety, insomnia, high blood pressure and a weakened immune system, depression, obesity and heart disease (www.apa.org)

It is vital that we look for ways to reduce stress in our workplace so that these side effects do not become present in our lives. The many forms of coping with this stress can make life even more difficult. Many people resort to overeating (stress eating), eating unhealthy foods, smoking, alcohol, drugs, and other habits that breed anxiety. Not only are these dangerous, but they also cause us to harm others and lose any positive influence we may have.

When we look at our current circumstances at work, what are we trying to achieve? Is our goal to be average? Is our goal to be just as good as those around us? Are we constantly working to meet the status quo, punch the time clock, and get out as soon as possible? If the answer to these questions is "yes," we will still have an influence on those we work with; it just won't be a positive influence.

In my previous jobs, my mindset was not what it should have been. I tried to come up with things other people could do to make my job easier or better. I tried to change people so that they could be more beneficial to me in the workplace. Perhaps one of the greatest lessons I learned from this experience is this: We can't change people; we can only change ourselves. If we want to grow, if we want to reduce anxiety, WE must change. Admitting we need to change is hard. Changing ourselves is even harder. However, when we are willing to change, we will have a greater influence on others. Our actions speak so much louder than our words.

> *We can't change people; we can only change ourselves.*

We must keep in mind the words of Paul to the church at Colosse, "*Whatever you do, do it heartily, as to the Lord and not to men, knowing that from the Lord you will receive the reward of the inheritance; for you serve the Lord Christ*" (Colossians 3:23 – 24). What if Jesus was our boss? Would we work differently? Would our attitude change? Would we be more helpful to others? Let's challenge ourselves this week to imagine we are working for Jesus, not the person we call boss. Make note of the influence we have through our positive outlook and service to others.

To reduce stress at my job, I learned to look for the aspects I did enjoy and focus my attention there. I did my best to bring joy to my co-workers and the customers I saw on a regular basis. When I struggled to take the attention off myself, I was allowing the opportunity for stress to stick around. Because stress levels nearly always decreased when I was helping someone other than myself, I spent time looking for ways to help others. I was amazed at the opportunities I was given because of my changed outlook. In the last few months of that job, I was offered some important positions with other companies. These were opportunities offered to me by our customers and would have more than doubled my salary. I could have afforded the car I had always wanted. I began putting together a résumé that made me look like I was a very important and qualified person. In the middle of this process, I got a phone call that would change my career path forever.

There was a little church in Louisiana that had been looking for someone to work in a non-profit ministry called Spanish Missions. They had been looking for several years but hadn't found someone who met all the requirements they were asking of the potential candidate. A friend of mine, who had learned of this job, called me to see if I was interested, and to give me the phone number to call so I could inquire about the position. I had the opportunity to interview over the phone with the director of the ministry who had also started the ministry about 35 years earlier (several years before I had been born).

Part of the conversation was a little awkward because he asked if he could speak to me in Spanish for a few minutes and I agreed. I listened to him speak and was in awe how a man from Louisiana spoke flawless Spanish. Clearly, this was not the first time he had spoken the language. When he finished, all I could muster up was, "I understood what you said, but I don't really have anything to add." I was quite the conversationalist! The following day, he sent me an email outlining the job responsibilities, requirements, and the commitment they were looking for. It was two pages of single-spaced content. I believe it was written to scare me off. I don't say this because I think he didn't like me but because they were serious about finding someone and didn't want to leave out any details or expectations...and they didn't.

After reading the email, I was still thinking about my other opportunities. There was one I considered that had a starting salary of three times the amount the Spanish ministry job was going to pay. It was to be the director of customer service for a large insurance company. At times, I wonder what would have happened if I had taken that job. I would probably have a lot more money, but I truly believe I would have much less purpose. After much consideration, I decided to take the Spanish Missions job.

Getting rid of stress demands change in our life. Growth on every level requires change in some capacity. This isn't the first time I have mentioned this, and it won't be the last. I hope it sticks! Sometimes, we look forward to change because it can be fun and easy. Other times, it brings a level of uncertainty that causes pressure and stress that create anxiety in our life that lead to other illness. Many people settle for mediocrity in their occupation because they don't know or don't think they can use their talents within their job. This is not true! We all have talents and should look for ways to incorporate them into our jobs. When we use our talents and enjoy what we do, work doesn't seem like work. It's hard to have anxiety when you are having fun.

Every day, I wake up looking forward to the opportunities to be presented to me through my job. When I started in 2008, we had 2,300 students enrolled in our online Spanish bible courses. We now have over 30,000 students enrolled and average more than 2.6 million downloads per month. This is in addition to the thousands of Facebook messages we get each month and the 1,200 students that study with us via regular postal mail. There are only two of us working in this ministry to take care of all the online administration and correspondence. We have the option to be overwhelmed or to get up each morning and enjoy the opportunity to take care of the needs of so many who are looking for what we offer. As I mentioned earlier in the chapter, stress levels decrease when we are helping people other than ourselves.

If you don't currently have your dream job, can you make it your dream job? In your profession, are you currently helping to make the lives of your co-workers or employees easier? What can you do to serve those around you? When you feel your stress levels rise, find someone to help. It is much like the antidote for discouragement. When you feel discouraged, go encourage someone.

Whether you are looking for a job, just getting started in a job, or have been in the same profession for many years, you can use T.R.I.A.L.S. to help reduce the stress in your day-to-day life at work. For those looking for a job, I suggest asking yourself, "Can I incorporate these qualities into the lives of people around me?" This will serve more as a stress prevention instead of stress reducer. For those looking to reduce stress, the process of starting to implement the T.R.I.A.L.S. method can be a little awkward, but after the initial awkwardness, the benefits of this method will soon be seen in your relationships in your job.

Let's get practical with T.R.I.A.L.S. In all your work-related stress, can you display the following characteristics? As you will see, the key to every one of these qualities is communication. Sit down and analyze each of these areas and look for ways to improve or change yourself to help reduce stress. You may already be some of these things and only need help in one or two areas. Make goals. Be reasonable. Be proactive.

Transparency – Before understanding what this means, it is important to understand what it doesn't mean. It DOES NOT mean we lose our filter. Our speech should always bring grace to those to whom we speak (see Colossians 4:6). We should communicate with a calm spirit as often as possible, even when it is difficult. Develop an "I can" attitude.

Can you be open and honest with your boss, co-workers, and employees? One of the keys to great leadership is transparency. Whether you are the leader or the follower, you must clearly communicate your expectations of others and yourself. Don't keep secrets. They cause stress.

Answer these questions: Am I doing all I can to clearly communicate on the job? How can I improve?

Would I rather live with the anxiety that comes with secrets/dishonesty or the vulnerability that comes from being transparent? Great leaders are transparent. Choose greatness.

Responsibility – Do you own your actions or are you making excuses and blaming others for problems at work? Part of accepting responsibility is admitting when we are wrong or need to improve. As we create a transparent atmosphere in the workplace, accepting responsibility for our actions is the next step in reducing stress at work.

Think of one thing, perhaps the most important thing, at work that you need to admit or improve. Now, take the next step to create change and see how positive change reduces stress.

Intentionality – Stress reduction is not going to happen on accident and neither will the rest of these qualities. Ephesians 5:15 – 17 teaches how we should live with purpose in making the best use of our time. When we choose to think and give purpose to our words and decisions, the result is usually better than when we are forced to react. Being intentional allows us to be proactive instead of reactive. In our career, if we make a habit of being intentional with our time and our energy, we leave a better lasting impression on those around us. We will also gain opportunity to prevent stress as well as reduce it.

Appreciation – Two of the most unused words in the English language are "thank you." Unless someone is receiving a gift, these words may never get used and maybe not even then (depending on the person). If we are going to commit to being transparent, responsible, and intentional, the next step to decreasing stress and eliminating anxiety is living a life of gratitude. Appreciation creates positivity and makes people smile. Not only will this create a better environment for everyone, but it will reduce stress between people when they appreciate each other. We all work better when we feel appreciated.

Colossians 3:15 – 17 tells us to let Christ rule in our hearts and to be thankful. Think of one person who really needs to hear how much she/he is needed and appreciated at work. Be the person to show gratitude. Create an attitude of gratitude among all your colleagues and enjoy the positive environment you create.

Limits – We all have limits. If you are overwhelmed, you may be pushing or exceeding your personal limits of what you can handle at work. Make a list of your responsibilities and figure out how you can eliminate or delegate so that you don't add undue stress. As a minister, I get asked to do a lot. At times, it is more than I can handle, but I still have a hard time saying "no" when someone asks me to lead another Bible study or teach another class. We need to remember every time we say yes to something, we are saying "no" to something else. Know your limits and learn to avoid putting more on your plate than you can handle. This requires us to be transparent with ourselves.

Even the great apostle Paul had limits. He couldn't do everything. In Philippians 2, he sent the best help he had to the church at Philippi to do what he could not. We would do well to follow his example in understanding when we can and can't achieve something on our own.

Simplify – We homeschool our kids. A while back, I was teaching our oldest daughter fractions and how 8/4 is equal to 4/2 is equal to 2/1. There are times when a project looks bigger than it is. The key to simplifying at work is figuring out what is necessary and what is not. We may have some habits or tasks we do just for the sake of doing them and they cost us a lot of time. Evaluate your responsibilities and habits and make sure the things you are doing are necessary. Who knows how much time you can save and how much more productive you can be?

This does not mean to get rid of ALL our responsibilities. The word "reduce" means to make smaller. This is the goal with stress, but one of the ways we reduce stress is reducing things that bring stress. If you have too much on your plate, think of one thing you can delegate to someone else, ask for help accomplishing it, or perhaps find one thing on your plate that may not be necessary at all. This will help you at work. When we look at finances, it will be overwhelming how much simplifying reduces stress.

Motivation: Focus on the area of your job that gives you the most stress/anxiety. Set aside at least five minutes before each work day and determine to find a way to serve someone involved in this area that gives you stress. Or, find someone else who may be dealing with a stressful situation and help him/her through it.

Advice: Work your job as if God was your boss and Jesus was your co-worker. Watch morale soar!

Prayer: Lord, help me to set my mind on heavenly things. Relieve me of the anxiety I choose to hang on to when stress is overwhelming. Strengthen my mind and give me the courage and confidence I need to overcome weakness.

Chapter 6 – Finances and Anxiety

I was recently asked to co-teach a class on marriage and family. We were covering areas from dating to death and everything in between. In the last 11 years, I have had the opportunity to teach on a wide variety of topics, including this one. In fact, I have taught on marriage and family in several countries in South and Central America. I should have had no reservations about teaching this class. When I was a newlywed, I taught a class on marriage and even covered the topic of sex and marriage and didn't feel uncomfortable teaching a group of people older than myself.

I learned quickly I would rather teach about sex than money. Why? Most of us can laugh at ourselves and especially at an awkward teacher when it comes to talking about intimacy. It is easier to make jokes and be a little light-hearted and still maintain a focus when talking about how we should treat our spouses. However, when it comes to talking about finances, the majority are sensitive to feeling everyone knows their budget, income and how they spend their money. We would rather not talk about the topic at all than to let someone know how much we spent on dinner last night or the car we bought last month. What does this tell us about money? It can be one of the biggest causes of anxiety in our lives!

Oddly enough, not only was I given the topic of finances in the home, I was also given the topic of marriage, divorce, and re-marriage. The two most common causes cited for divorce I found in all my research were communication and finances. What are we to learn from this research? If we all talk a lot and have lots of money, will we have successful marriages? Clearly, this is not the case! Our view of money and stress can determine a great deal of who we are and how we will treat ourselves and others.

Because we all come from different backgrounds, our view on money is going to be different. It is difficult, perhaps impossible, to come up with a "one-size fits all" formula to pinpoint where finances have caused anxiety and how to solve this problem. This chapter is not intended to offer a solution to those under the poverty line to become wealthy or accuse them of being poor stewards. It is not to address problems between socio-economic classes of individuals. My hope is to help us all be more fiscally responsible, have a healthier view of money, and understand how it affects our stress levels.

As we begin our journey of reducing stress and eliminating anxiety relative to our finances, I want us to keep in mind principles we have already looked at regarding normalcy and comparative living. Unfortunately, when it comes to our finances, many of us have anxiety because we value the opinions of others and what they think of how we earn an income, how much income we earn and how we spend it.

Why do we worry about finances? Is it because we want more for our families than we had growing up? Is it because of bills we must pay? Nearly everything we do requires us to have money. Our food, clothes, entertainment, utilities, etc. Hardly anything is free in life!

We view money and possessions in several different ways, and each has positive and negative potential when moderation is not practiced. When I was a kid, I was commonly referred to as the miser in the family. I remember when one of my dad's friends came to the house and gave all the kids a pack of starburst or my grandparents would give us M&Ms. I would wait until everyone had finished their candy before I even started eating mine. I loved to save. I did this with money also. I don't know why I managed what I was given the way I did, but it worked for me. As a kid, debt didn't mean anything to me, but saving what I had meant I could enjoy it longer. For all the other kids, there was something about instant gratification. Now, as a father of four, I can see which of my kids have the "miser" gene and which ones prefer the instant gratification. I sit back and laugh as I'm sure my parents did when I was growing up.

When I was in junior high, I learned a priceless lesson from my cousin. He knew I saved my money and I was willing to work hard for money. He also knew I was on top of the world if I found money or won money in a contest of any sort. I remember being with him on one occasion and seeing a ten-dollar bill on the ground. I would have dived on it if anyone else had been going for it. When I had the bill in my hand, I shouted "Yes!" My overwhelming excitement must have struck him in a less than positive way. He told me I placed way too much value on money. I thought, "That's easy for you to say. You don't have to worry about money." Do any of us *have to* worry about money?   It was then my perspective began to change. At the time, I didn't realize what an impact this would have on me years later.

Fast forward to the college years and things didn't change much. I worked hard each summer before returning to the dorm life I cherished. I worked one or two jobs during the summer and would save most of what I earned so that I could have fun while I was in school. For me, fun meant eating out a few times a week. I was on a meal plan that allowed me to eat three meals a day in the cafeteria. While I loved the cafeteria food, I also loved playing soccer and spending hours in the weight room every day. This combination along with a very high metabolism meant I was going to be hungry outside of the cafeteria hours. Unfortunately, I did not manage my funds as well as I should have during these years. I learned there is a difference between not being anxious about money and being responsible at the same time.

In fact, at the end of my sophomore year, I had managed my money so poorly I relied on the money I received from selling my books back to the bookstore to put gas in my truck, so that I could make the four-hour drive home. As soon as I got home, I knew mom would feed me, fill my truck with gas and I would be able to get back to work so that I could have the security I felt when I had money in my bank account. Thankfully, I did not get a credit card when I was in college. This was one of the greatest blessings during my college experience. We will discuss credit cards later in this chapter. If I didn't have money in the bank to buy something, I couldn't buy it.

I have seen funny skits on late night shows about the odd idea of buying things when we don't have the money to pay for them. Tim Clue is a comedian with an entire routine on debt. It is one of the funniest acts I have seen. When you have time, search for Tim Clue and debt on the internet. Sit back and get ready to laugh at the truth behind the sad reality he portrays in such a funny way. You won't be disappointed. Our society isn't in financial ruin by accident but because we have allowed it to become this way. Therefore, financial stress becomes the next customer in line to launch itself into our lives.

Financial anxiety isn't initiated by having an abundance of money and possessions, nor is it initiated by having very little wealth. If you search through studies on financial stress, you will find (in most cases) one in ten Americans does not feel financial stress. That's a staggering statistic for those who are in the ninety percent column and sobering for those in the ten percent column. Is financial ruin one bad decision? For some, perhaps one decision has created a terrible financial situation. However, for most, it is compounding one poor decision on top of another that has created a lifestyle of spending more than they earn. Most research groups show close to 50% of Americans run out of money before their next paycheck and only 41% use a budget. Maybe there is a correlation? Don't seek to be a statistic; be responsible.

1st Timothy 6 is a gold mine for us when it comes to our perspective on money. The concept driven in this chapter deals with the eternal race that consumes our existence. It's about life, both the physical and the spiritual. We are told to "take hold of the eternal life to which we have been called." For us to take hold of something, we must let go of whatever it is we are clinging to. Our focus must be spiritual. In verse 10 of this chapter, Paul says the love of money is the root of all sorts of evil. I believe this to be more true today than ever.

When I was 12 years old, I started a house cleaning business. Why? Because I loved money. I didn't really care if people lived in clean houses. I wanted money and so I found ways to make as much of it as I could, and I made good money cleaning. I had to learn to change my focus and my perspective on money.

Why do we love money so much? Is it natural? Is it something we can't help? There are several reasons we may love money. I hope this book helps you to understand that regardless of which area in life causes you stress, you have the power to change. You can change your attitude. You can change your perspective. If money is something that causes you anxiety, change is a must. So many tools and resources are available to us to help us have a healthier view of money and reduce anxiety at the same time. See the recommended readings at the end of the book for some of these resources.

Unfortunately, our culture makes it so difficult to be fiscally responsible. We are constantly surrounded by people and companies telling us how much we need the latest greatest _____. How ironic is it our country has put "in God we trust" on the very thing we trust more than God?

How does this make sense? Do we trust more in the power of the dollar which consumes so many of us or the power of God who says He will provide for us?

In Deuteronomy 8:18, we read God gives us the power to make money or gain wealth. We certainly have a responsibility to work and provide for ourselves and our families. When I think of all the people in history, I don't know of anyone more blessed than the man named Job we read about in the Old Testament. Why was he so blessed? I believe it had a great deal to do with the fact his focus was not his possessions but rather his trust in God.

> "The rich rule over the poor and the borrower becomes slave to the lender" – Proverbs 22:7

Nothing is wrong with having money or possessions. However, when our desire becomes our love of the creation instead of the Creator, we have problems. We will experience anxiety. The Bible is our most valuable resource when it comes to how we should view and use money.

One of the most challenging verses in relationship to money and debt is found in Proverbs 22:7. It says, "The rich rule over the poor and the borrower becomes slave to the lender." I can't think of anyone who wants to be a slave. This principle should change the way we borrow and lend money. Perhaps this is the verse so many financial consultants have used for their teaching on not living in debt. It is the driving force behind one of the principles we live by in our family. "If you can't afford it, don't buy it."

> "If you can't afford it, don't buy it!"

Don't be a slave to debt! At the same time, the principle is just as important when it comes to lending money. Any time we lend money to someone, that one becomes our slave.

If you don't believe this, lend someone money and try not to micromanage every financial decision they make until they pay you back. How would you feel if you loaned someone $500 because they said they didn't have money to pay their bills? They promised to pay you back $100 per month for 5 months. You weren't interested in collecting interest because, for you, it wasn't that big of a deal. After all, you just want to help them. Imagine running into them at the bowling alley or some other extracurricular activity and watch them spend $200 on something frivolous when they still owe you money. It's hard to watch, and it creates tension and stress between us and our friends or family when we lend them money. My opinion has changed to this: If I can't afford to give money to the person in need, I don't give it.

For the most part, our culture is consumed with a desire to have more stuff. Commercialism is at an all-time high. Savings plans, 401(K), bonuses are all parts of salary packages that are supposed to appeal to a job applicant more than the job that pays only enough to provide for one's needs. It would be difficult to turn down the higher paying job for one that just meets our needs. Perhaps you are thinking right now how much nicer it would be to have a job that provided better financial stability. However, if we are honest with ourselves, we could probably have the financial peace and stability in our current situation if we learned to live within our means or perhaps even under our means. How can we understand this concept? Living within our means is a simple concept, but it requires us to have a good memory or to take notes. My suggestion is taking notes. Make a budget.

Credit cards may or may not have come from the devil. Credit cards seem to exist to ruin financial peace for people in our country. When I was in college, it was common to see credit card companies set up around campus trying to get students to sign up. They were giving away a whole pizza to everyone who would just stop by and give them a name and phone number. If I'm honest, I probably would have given more than that for the pizza! I didn't think I was allowed to have a credit card, so I was happy to give them information if I didn't have to sign the application. I had several friends who were happy to sign the application and get the approval of these fine institutions to borrow their money. At a 27% interest rate, they were going to be fine!

The only time I can recall having financial anxiety in my life is a time when I would have used a credit card if I had had one. I can recall preparing to come home at the end of a semester in college and not having enough money in the bank to put gas in my tank. As I mentioned earlier, I resorted to selling back my books to the university for a few hundred dollars so that I could eat and make it home. These are books I paid thousands for! But, at that time, it didn't matter what they had cost me if they could get me home.

I get credit card offers every week in the mail. Without a doubt, some great benefits come from using credit cards for rewards and paying them off each month. In fact, these rewards are the only way our family can afford to travel from time to time outside of the state we live in. In fact, I'm editing the final draft of this book while I'm on a flight to California with my bride. Our flight and hotel stay are completely paid for by reward points. However, credit card companies never lose. If you don't have the self-control to buy only what you can afford, my suggestion is not to have the credit card.

As I mentioned earlier, the purpose of this chapter is not to increase your wealth, but rather to decrease your levels of anxiety that come from finances. Do principles that reduce stress apply to those who have plenty of money and those that have hardly any? The answer is YES! Is it easier for one group than it is the other? This is a question that can be answered only by the person following the principles.

If you get time, I encourage you to read Ecclesiastes 5:8 - 20 for a list of principles and another way money should be viewed.

A few months after we were married, our bills started coming in and the payment on the $80,000 I had borrowed for college was not pretty. Shortly before accepting my current job, I had a few job offers that would have paid a six figure income. My wife was also waiting for a job offer from a pharmaceutical sales company that would have paid more than I was going to make. Do you think my first thought was paying off all the college debt? Not even close! We didn't have kids and I wanted a sports car. It didn't matter if I could afford it. If I could finance it, I could buy it. This principle characterizes most of our culture. With the income we anticipated, we could have borrowed $600,000 for a house on top of the cars we wanted to drive. We were on track to be slaves to the bank and financial institutions for the rest of our lives. Thankfully, I married a very sensible woman!

The key to understanding the text we looked at in chapter one (Matthew 6:25 – 34) is looking at the verse that comes immediately before verse 25. Jesus says, "*No one can serve two masters.*" If we desire to live without anxiety that comes from finances, we cannot love money. We must love God first, not just in word or thought, but in action.

Other benefits come from not being self-focused when it comes to our finances. In 1 Timothy 5:8, we also have a responsibility to provide for our own. Paul uses some of the strongest language to describe someone who does not take care for his family. He says they are worse than an unbeliever.

1st John 3:17 teaches us, *"But if anyone has the world's goods and sees his brother in need, yet closes his heart against him, how does God's love abide in him?"*

A key to understanding these verses is knowing we must take care of ourselves before we can take care of other people. I know people who are generous to a fault. They may barely have enough to cover their own expenses, but if they see someone in need, they would borrow money to help someone out and then tack that on to their own personal debt. I don't believe this is the way God wants us to live.

There are also some who have no financial worries at all. How does the person who has more than enough respond to financial responsibility? Keep reading in 1 Timothy 6:17 – 19. In short, those with more money than they need, have a responsibility to help those who do not. They are also instructed to enjoy what they have. Period. If this is the category you find yourself in, enjoy your well-being and help those in need. It is not meant for us to enable people, but to help with the NEEDS of others.

I want to share two key principles with you that have been helpful to my family in reducing money-related stress and anxiety.

Principle #1 - Money doesn't make you rich, perception does

I haven't done the research to show which category of statistics you are in based on your current financial situation. In fact, I haven't done the research to figure out what statistical category I belong in either because it really doesn't matter. Your income, your family size, your expenses, etc. are personal to you as mine are to me. I want to share with you some personal information and how my wife and I have been able to use these two principles to overcome a large amount of debt and maintain a healthy marriage with very little financial stress and anxiety. Not everyone will have the same opportunities we have had to get rid of our debt. Some have greater opportunities and some less. I hope my story is helpful to you.

My bride and I said "I Do" about two months after we graduated college. We moved to Arkansas with plans to get jobs and start living the American dream. We had no idea what was ahead for us. We lived with my parents for eight months while deciding to rent, buy or build a house. Due to the jobs we were offered, we decided to build. It was nice of the bank to allow us to move in and not make our first mortgage payment until 45 days after we closed. It was like living in a new house for a month and not having to pay for it. We didn't know we would be paying for it on the back end. When the first payment was due, I decided to sit down and create a budget for our family, which would be only the two of us for about another year.

I'm still not sure how we survived financially for the first year of our marriage. I graduated from a private school. Even with two different scholarships, I was strapped with $858 per month of student loan payments. The good news was it was only on a 15-year term. At this rate, my $80,000 education was only going to cost me a meager $154,400 by the time it was all said and done unless I found a way to pay them off earlier. Those interest rates were making someone rich and it wasn't me!

We were fortunate to build a nice home and stay on budget to keep our mortgage payment slightly lower than my student loan payments. What a blessing that was! Of course, the kind mortgage people failed to escrow our taxes, so we received a mortgage bump of $200 per month after the first six months. I felt like we were handed one of the community chest cards on a Monopoly board and not one of the good ones!

There we sat in our living room one night trying to make all the numbers make sense. I had just changed jobs and received a decent pay raise. I was bringing home about $700/week. Kristen was still waiting to hear back on a job opportunity and was contemplating furthering her education, which was a requirement for a different job she was investigating. If we pause and do some quick math, there was a short time when we were clearing $2,800/month and spending $1,800 on our mortgage and student loans. That left us $1,000/month to buy insurance, a small car note, cell phones, food and utilities. I'm not sure how we afforded to eat. Although, I do remember so many romantic dates at the Taco Bell where we split a grilled stuffed burrito and glass of water. It's hard to beat a $3.30 date! Now, I can't imagine what would happen if we ate at a Taco Bell, but it wouldn't be pretty . . . wait for the chapter on health and stress!

I would like to say we were financially prepared for the first year of marriage, but we weren't even close. We had high hopes of going on extravagant dates and traveling as we did on our honeymoon, which was at someone else's expense. Even though we were unprepared for the bills that were coming our way, I don't recall a tremendous amount of stress due to our financial situation. We hadn't been irresponsible. We weren't purchasing outlandish items of any sort. There were a couple of lessons we had to learn through experience. These experiences allowed us to understand you can be fiscally responsible and not be stressed out at the same time.

Our goal was happiness not wealth. Our view of money was simple. It is a tool. It paid bills. It helped people. We needed money, but we did not love money. We were barely able to pay our bills, but we were able. If you ask me if we were rich during our first year of marriage, I would say absolutely! It's not about how much you make: it's about how you manage what you have. At the time, I had a negative net worth and still felt like one of the richest men alive! That means if I were to have sold everything I owned and added it to the cash I had in the bank and then subtracted all my debt, I would have been worth a negative $100,000. Feeling good!

I was as happy and content then as I am now, and my net worth is in the positive. How am I able to be rich if I am worth a negative $100,000 or a positive $100,000? Perception! My net worth is not $1,000,000 but if it was, I would like to think my perception of money wouldn't change. If we place our value in money, we will need lots of money to feel valuable. If we place our value in family, faith, friendships and experiences, being rich is much more attainable and much less stressful.

Principle #2 – Possessions need purpose

The second principle can be more difficult to appreciate. It has to do with giving purpose to possessions. At first glance, this may not sound that challenging. However, if you had to sit down in a room with nothing and make a list of everything you NEEDED, how long would your list be? Would it extend past food, clothing and shelter? What if you had to sell or get rid of everything you didn't need? Be thankful you don't have to do either!

A few years ago, my bride read a book about minimalism and it changed the way we looked at possessions. Reading the book caused us to want to learn more from people who lived a minimalistic lifestyle. Two guys who call themselves the minimalists travel the country talking to people about benefits of living with less. It is hard to argue with the majority of what they have to say.

I want to challenge us to all give purpose to our possessions. We may not be able to change purchases we have already made, but if we start where we are right now, our future will be much brighter and less stressful. The average American home has 300,000 items in it. How many do we have? Do we need everything in our house? When I first read this fact, I thought "I'm not even close to 300,000," but the more I analyzed, the less impressed I was with what I owned.

One of the big changes our family has made in the last few years is getting rid of our excess. We have built several houses which means we have moved several times. In eleven years of marriage, we have had thirteen addresses. This includes five apartments. When you move that many times, you learn a lot about what you need and don't need. One of the greatest lessons we have learned came when we were in an apartment for three months. We brought everything we needed to the apartment and put all our excess in storage while we were building. When we finished building our house, we realized if we didn't need the stuff we had in storage for three months, we didn't need it at all. At that point, we began to reevaluate our possessions and which of them had purpose and which did not.

We have so much in our house we don't need that someone else may genuinely need. No one needs ten pairs of shoes or twelve pairs of dress shorts. That's right, I had twelve pairs of dress shorts in one drawer!! When we look at our clothes alone, we see so much excess. I got rid of half of my wardrobe and still felt I had more than I needed. Every year, I go through my dresser and look at the shirts I own. If there is a shirt I didn't wear in the previous year, I get rid of it.

One of the challenges that comes with a wardrobe goes back to what we discussed in chapter one. We place so much value on what others think of our clothes. We stress out making sure we don't wear the same outfit twice in one week unless we are certain we aren't going to bump into someone we saw when we wore it the first time. I preach nearly every Sunday. I like to dress up when I speak. I own two suits and 6 ties. I used to worry about changing my shirt tie combo every week to make it look like I was wearing something different than the previous week. I've learned people don't really care about my clothes that much, if at all. I know I don't pay enough attention to what others wear each week to notice if they are wearing something they wore the week before. This could be partly because I have four kids, but the truth is I don't care if someone has only one set of "church" clothes. It makes me no difference.

Commercialism also makes it difficult to minimize possessions or give value to them. We decided years ago to get rid of cable to shield our kids from the many things television tells them they need. They have more toys than they need but still don't have much. Any time they want to purchase something new, we have them choose at least one or more toys to get rid of. This makes it much easier to get rid of the clutter and keep it from accumulating in our house.

Living in a digital age also helps us avoid clutter. We have a few hard copies of pictures and picture books, but most of our keep sakes are on a hard drive, computer, or in a cloud. We use a few pictures along with minimal furnishings to decorate our house. We are not overly sentimental about any of our possessions which aids us in giving them purpose.

We have also simplified our kitchen. Before we had kids, we owned enough china and dishware to feed 40 people. I can remember how many times we needed all those dishes. None. Zero. There was never an occasion when we were feeding that many people so why did we have all those dishes? It wasn't until a few years ago we realized we were allowed to get rid of the dishes we didn't need or use. There are many people who would love to have some quality dishes and we found someone with a need and donated them. I'm pretty sure we were happier to get rid of the dishes than the recipients were to receive them.

Learning to minimize possessions and give purpose to what we have can be a difficult transition for many reasons. We like stuff. We are trained to like stuff. Our kids like stuff. You get the idea. When we get rid of stuff we like, it can seem self-deprecating. We also are concerned what will happen if we get rid of an item that was gifted to us from a close friend or, especially, a family member. Recently, my wife was giving a seminar on decluttering the home and mind. During the seminar, she was explaining how we don't have to keep gifts we didn't ask to receive. We don't have to keep gifts we do ask for either, especially if they no longer have a purpose. When she received concerned looks from audience members, she said, "I give you permission to get rid of things in your home you are keeping around just because someone gave them to you." The look of relief on some of the faces must have been priceless.

> *Having less is more liberating than you can imagine.*

I am not a hoarder. On any given Sunday, you will catch me in one of three outfits. That recently changed when I lost my pants in the airport. You won't find a closet full of clothes in my house. Having less is more liberating than you can imagine. If you don't believe that, I challenge you to give it a try. Soon, you will find more purpose in what you do have.

My parents and my in-laws have come to learn to really think before they buy us anything. Because we don't hang onto much, and we don't like for them to waste their money, we have encouraged them not to buy us or the kids material gifts unless they are practically beneficial. This past Christmas, for the first time, we focused on experience giving, not gift giving. It has been the most rewarding season in our marriage. My parents are giving sewing lessons and project building lessons to my kids. Others are getting special one-on-one dates with Mimi or Nana instead of a toy they might use for ten minutes. Gifts of time and educational moments are so much more valuable than stuff. I would encourage us all to think about how to minimize the excess so that we have a greater appreciation for the possessions we need in our life.

One of the great challenges we face today is teaching the next generation the importance of financial responsibility and foresight. We are trying to do this in our house by teaching our kids the need to invest time in their future before they invest money. Most high school age kids prepare themselves to go to college within the first few months of when they receive their diploma. Many kids receive scholarships of some sort and even a few receive full ride scholarships. This leaves the majority left to borrow tens of thousands of dollars to receive an education that may or may not help them in their journey on an uncertain career path.

What if we were to help our kids gain as much experience as possible in as many different areas of interest so that they can learn what their passions are while they are in high school. What if when they graduate, we encourage them to volunteer in their fields of interests and get internships if possible, so that they can learn what career they want to pursue. So many people graduate college unsure of what they want to do or without a plan. One of my college roommates graduated with a degree in human resource management. Every job he applied for wanted a college graduate with a minimum of five years of experience. How do you get experience without opportunity? Our plan is to seek out opportunity before we invest in education. Perhaps our children will find a way for their employer to pay for their school while they are working? Either way, we must teach the next generation the importance of planning ahead with education and finances. I don't wish an $80,000 education debt on anyone who can only find a job starting out at $30,000/year. Those numbers won't ever add up!

The last area I want to briefly mention about money before we look at the T.R.I.A.L.S. method is benevolence. From the beginning of time, God has always been a giver. In fact, He has always been the best example of generosity known to man. When we consider ways for us to give back, I hope we always keep in mind the principles we have looked at. We must take care of ourselves, our families, and then others, especially those who belong to God. It is also important for our attitude to match our actions. If our giving to God or others causes us anxiety, we need to reconsider our attitude toward the gift. Money is a tool God has leant us to help ourselves and help others. Let's make sure we use it wisely!

Regardless of your current situation, the greatest keys to preventing money-related anxiety in marriage can be found in T.R.I.A.L.S. If all the steps are followed, we may not be rich, but we won't have to wonder where all our money goes. Each one of these characteristics must be clearly communicated between those involved in a financial union. Whether you are single or in a relationship, these six qualities must exist to reduce financial stress and eliminate anxiety.

Transparency – There can be no secrets when it comes to finances. We must be honest with ourselves and honest with our spouses. Some of the greatest problems arise when we make purchases that affect others and they don't know about them. We must make every effort to communicate our financial decisions to those whom they affect. No one likes to be blindsided in any situation, especially with money.

If you want to be practical, make a budget and try to be as exact as you can. Write down your income and then write down an itemized list of expenses. Don't write what you want them to be, but write down what they are exactly. Get bank statements and credit card statements and see how much you actually spend on food, clothing, shelter, utilities, entertainment, hobbies, etc. You may be surprised and maybe even disappointed at where all your money goes. I know I was when I first put a budget together! The key to getting our finances under control and eliminating stress starts with an understanding of how we spend our money and its purpose. If you do this before you marry, you have a huge head start and it will be a great blessing to your future spouse. If you are married, it is never too late to start making a budget. If we can't be honest with ourselves, we won't be honest with others and we will have anxiety!

Responsibility – Owning our decisions from the past and present is vital. If we have debt, we must pay it back. We must understand the need to think before we spend because some financial decisions can have lifelong consequences. Just as creating a budget helps with transparency, it really helps with responsibility. Being responsible also means we stick to the budget we create. When transparency is coupled with responsibility, the next key in reducing stress is intentionality.

Intentionality – Being intentional has to do with purpose and planning. If we will be intentional with the way we spend money, there won't be any "accidental" purchases. Every purchase we make needs to be thought out well enough that it isn't going to affect our budget and finances in a negative way. If we make a plan for our finances and stick to the plan, reduced stress will be the result. If shopping is a coping mechanism, find a new one! Make sure there is a purpose to your purchase!

Appreciation – When people are willing to be transparent, responsible, and intentional, there must be appreciation. It isn't always easy to be transparent and make responsible decisions. Develop an attitude of gratitude. When you or someone else communicates and commits to these first three qualities, reducing financial stress can become a fun adventure which leads us to understanding our limits.

Limits – We all have them. The wealthiest person in the world and the man who owns nothing more than the shirt on his back both have limits. The key to understanding limits is space. We find ourselves in trouble when we push limits financially. The greatest benefit of steering clear of financial limits is having a little left at the end of the month to help someone in need. The greatest stress reducer in my life has been helping others. It may be helping them donate time and energy, but money is also a need that many people have, especially if they have gone through a tragedy. We may have to do without or sacrifice some of our "fun money" to help someone, but the decrease in stress is far more valuable than the fun we might have experienced.

Simplify – Stress is the result of too much. Whether it is too much stuff we own, too much responsibility we have, too much authority we have been given, too much _____. Stress comes when we feel we can't handle the load on our back and the pressure seems insurmountable. Finding ways to detox or simplify the pressures of life will help reduce stress that comes from too much of anything.

When we consider work and finances together, we need to ask the question, "Why do I work so much?" If we are working more hours or we are in constant search of a higher paying job, so we can make more money to pay for more stuff, perhaps we should consider our most valuable asset. TIME. If we can challenge ourselves to simplify life and not crave so much stuff, we will have more time to enjoy the stuff we already have and the people around us. If we are working to pay for things we "had to have" that are financed, maybe we should look into getting rid of some of our toys so that we don't have to work so hard to pay for them.

Start where you are. Use what you have. Do what you can.

Motivation: If you have several debts, make a plan to get rid of one debt. It may be a short-term plan or a long-term plan but make a plan. Stick to it. We must help ourselves before we can help others.

Find a way to use the resources you have to help someone who will never find out or who would not expect it.

Advice: If you can't afford it, don't buy it. Period.

Prayer: Lord, thank you for your generosity and provision. Help me to value people and eternity. Help me not to value the things of this world. Help me to be responsible for the decisions I have made in the past and help me to respect the present moment. May my steps be worship, may my thoughts be praise as I seek to be a good steward of the abundant blessings you have provided. Help me to be generous to others, not only when they ask but when I see a need. May You be glorified in my life. Amen.

Chapter 7 – Health and Anxiety

You won't find much said about A.J. Reb Materi. However, he is noted for having said "So many people spend their health gaining wealth, and then have to spend their wealth to regain their health" (https://www.goodreads.com/author/quotes/13609922.A_J_Reb_Materi). This is the sad reality so many workaholics find themselves living. Anxiety that results from the way we respond to stress in our personal life, jobs, marriage, kids and finances often leads us to poor health.

When I was a kid, I knew everything. EVERYTHING. Well, I knew everything except the things I didn't know. My parents can vouch for this. When it came to life, I knew what I wanted. At the age of 8, I remember telling my dad I wanted to be a body builder. I wanted to look like the guys we saw on ESPN who won the strongest man in the world competition. Like it was yesterday, I can hear my dad saying, "No you don't. You don't want to spend 6 hours a day in the gym and eat an insane amount of food every day." He had me convinced, at that time, he was right.

When I got to college, I had a renewed energy and heightened metabolism that took me back to my young desire to be a body builder. My thought process was so far off. For most high school and college athletes, physical health is seen in a formula similar to: Protein = Good, Fat = Bad, Exercise = Good, Lazy = Bad.

I knew I could eat whatever I wanted if I worked it off in the gym. For 4 years, I spent 2 hours a day in the gym, so I could spend 2 hours a day in the cafeteria. Can you imagine the stress I put my body through? During this stint, I probably could have competed in body-building competitions, but I was far too busy to commit to anything of that nature.

The last year I was in college, I met the woman I desired to build my life around. I can't say enough about the many, many positive ways she changed my life. I have mentioned several of them in this book. Before I get into the specifics on how health and stress are related, the most important lesson I learned about physical health and stress is the role of genetics. Health and stress can be very subjective because everyone has a different genetic code. We all have doctors who give us different instructions for similar health and weight issues so that it becomes difficult to figure out the best path.

The most difficult challenge we face when it comes to our health and stress is the nature in which everyone of us is created. We all have a unique genetic makeup that makes it impossible to give the same protocol and medicinal instruction to two people with the same problem. What we are exposed to while we are in the womb and during our childhood plays a significant role in our development as we age. Some people have taken several kinds of medications for so long their immune systems don't respond the same as before.

When it comes to health and stress, we must first give a legitimate definition to the word healthy. When I was young, my definition of healthy meant skinny or athletic. Overweight didn't necessarily mean unhealthy, but it didn't carry a positive connotation either. I can remember setting a goal when I was 13 that I didn't want to become overweight. This goal was part of my motivation for playing sports. I realize not everyone can or wants to play sports, but we all need to have an exercise component in our health.

When I looked up the word "healthy" in Merriam-Webster's online dictionary, I was shocked to see how the word was defined. What stood out the most was the word disease. Healthy means free from disease (https://www.merriam-webster.com/dictionary/healthy).

Disease is a condition that impairs normal function. If we put it all together, healthy is simply avoiding things that impair our normal function.

> Healthy is simply avoiding things that impair our normal function.

There are several kinds of health, but for this chapter, we will focus on two components of physical health and how they relate to stress. If you have questions about mental, psychological and emotional health, T.R.I.A.L.S. can help you to some degree, but I suggest seeking out a professional who is qualified to give advice on the specific health needed.

We have two components to our physical health. Nutrition and exercise are the key elements that shape our bodies. Before we get into specifics on both topics, it is important to remember the greatest underlying factors in any nutrition goal or fitness plan is our genetics. Some people can't eat salt and others sugar. Some can eat bread and grains and others can't. Some bodies can run long distance and jump without joint pain. Other body types have trouble touching their toes or doing a squat. No one is smart enough to tell every person the best possible plan for their health based on their genetic code. For the remainder of this chapter, I want to share with you some principles that have worked for me the last several years. I hope they work for you as well.

Three of the most important questions to ask ourselves as we structure a diet or fitness plan that allows us to reduce stress in our lives are:

1. Does this help me prevent disease or will this make me healthier?
2. Is this sustainable in the long term?
3. If it works, am I willing to commit to this?

Physical Exercise

For the last two years, I have trained for the television show American Ninja Warrior. If you have never seen the show, it is an athletic competition in which tens of thousands of people audition and about 600 are selected to compete for a million dollars. The competition consists of obstacles that challenge your coordination, strength and endurance. Every morning, Monday through Friday, I go to the gym at 6:00 to work out and train. I am not following any routine someone has created. I make up my own workouts each week and push my body close to the limits of what it can handle. I have a training partner who helps with accountability, motivation and intensity during the workouts.

When we started this journey, we set a goal to complete ten sets of the following:

10 Pull-ups

100 Push-ups

10 Sit-ups (These are done wearing ankle boots and hanging upside down from a bar)

I was in pretty good shape when I started this kind of training, so it didn't take long before I reached the goal. I then set out to double the previous goal. After a few months, I was able to accomplish three times our original goal. All the tasks I wanted to complete I was able to finish.

I was getting stronger each week and any more increasing would potentially be too much strain on my body. One day, while visiting with my bride, we talked about the long-term benefits of this kind of training, and I was faced with a few tough choices. I loved my strength and endurance levels. I also ran on the weekends to keep my cardiovascular health in shape. However, when we looked at the three questions about healthy, sustainability and commitment, I realized only one of the three questions received a positive answer. Was my training helping me prevent disease? Yes. It's no secret that exercising increases your heart strength, helps blood flow, and lowers cholesterol. I also knew I could do much less intensity and still help my body prevent disease.

The next two questions did not get a positive response. Is this sustainable? No. This kind of training became a little extreme, and in the long-term, my body will not continue to increase production. When you feel you are in the prime of your life, you are able to perform the best. Regardless of which stage in life you are in, maintenance is important and should be considered when deciding on an exercise routine.

Like every area of growth in our life, we need a plan and we need commitment. Given that I feel good about my physical strength and health right now, I am willing to commit to the same exercises but not the same amount of repetitions and intensity. I need to slow down and make some healthy, attainable goals I can sustain for the long-term. Will I be able to reach these goals in ten years, twenty years, thirty years, etc.? Of course, goals can change based on many factors and variables that come along as we age. We need to learn how to maintain once we reach our goals.

What are your physical fitness goals? Do you have any? I am not a doctor or qualified to answer health-related questions. If you have questions about starting a workout routine and you are unsure of how and where to start, please consult your doctor. You may also want to consult a personal trainer to get started.

This is only half the equation and it is the easier half. Our bodies need exercise. They need to burn the fuel we ingest. We are all shaped differently and our bodies all react a little differently to the strain placed upon them. When I first started doing yoga, I remember the teacher saying, "Do what feels good in your body. If what you are doing doesn't feel good, back off and don't go so hard." This sounds simple enough, right? If we push ourselves to the limit and pain arises, we need to slow down and cut back if we want to prevent injuries. Has your body ever spoken to you? I know mine has, and it usually doesn't feel great when it is yelling at me!

Nutrition

The second half of the physical health equation is nutrition. Not everyone's body craves physical exercise, but we all need food for survival. Remember, the goal is to be healthy or free from disease. I recently saw a picture with a group of vegetables on one side and fried foods on the other. The caption read, "Everything we eat either fights disease or feeds disease." There is no middle ground. In this section, I am going to share with you my personal journey of how I have changed my diet and the benefits that came with these changes. I hope it helps you to understand growth is the result of change.

> *"Everything we eat either fights disease or feeds disease."*

Until we realize we have the power to change, we won't. When we understand we have the power to choose what we eat and how it affects our body, making healthier choices will make more sense. It isn't always easy, but if we want to reduce and eliminate anxiety that come from health, we will make the best choice.

Disclaimer – If you have already been diagnosed with a disease or illness that is affected by what you eat, please consult a nutritionist or doctor before following any diets that could be harmful to your body. Keep in mind, what works for one person may not work for another

As a little kid, I earned the nickname "Chunkadoo." I loved to eat just about everything. Like many kids, I didn't care much for green food or beans. I would go as far as saying I hated them. I was always grateful when my mom didn't force me to eat peas, and since she didn't like beans either, she rarely cooked them. When I was in junior high and high school, I ate enough food for someone twice my size. I can remember on some days after school, I would rush home to have dinner at my house. I would then go to a friend's house and have dinner with his family before we played basketball outside. I would end the evening at another friend's house and, often, would have dinner with them also. Three dinners? Yes, and I enjoyed each one!

Everyone in my family ate differently. My dad was a raw foodist for a few years. My mom didn't enjoy beans much, which was great, because I didn't either. My brother enjoyed eating a lot of meat which I did as well. My sister was a vegetarian for a while. During her time as a vegetarian, she bet me $100 I couldn't eat like a vegetarian for a year. It was late November when we made the bet. A few weeks later, I was playing in a basketball tournament and needed to get some food between games. My mom went with me to the concession stand, probably because she was buying. I told the worker I would like a chili-cheese dog, but then I remembered the bet and asked her not to put chili on it because chili had meat in it. It didn't even register with me that the hot dog was meat! Thankfully, my mom reminded me, and I decided on a healthier alternative. I had the nachos instead.

I also love Chinese food. It was the cheapest way to get the most food and the taste was hard to beat. I knew people that would order a plate of fried rice with meat and vegetables and would take it home and eat it for three different meals. For me, it would be only one meal and I would still be looking to find dessert between the restaurant and home. I couldn't get enough food! During one of the Christmas breaks when I was in college, I came home and ate so much Chinese food and worked out so hard, when I returned to school, the baseball coach asked me if I had been doing steroids over the break. That was good Chinese food!

The last eating story I will share took place on a trip to Colorado when I was in college. My dad and aunt, along with her two kids, made a trip to Denver to celebrate my grandparents 50th wedding anniversary. One evening, we stopped at Subway for dinner. They had a deal at that time, 3-foot-long subs for $10. That is a great deal! Instead of the three adults each picking one out and eating, I ordered three for myself while the other four people split three subs. Yes, I ate three foot long sandwiches by myself. My aunt didn't think I could do it, but I proved her wrong. I could share many more eating stories, but I think we get the point. I love to eat, a lot!

Why do I share these eating stories? My eating habits have changed drastically in 20 years. I used to think meat was needed at every meal. It is the only way to get protein in my diet, right? At times I preached at a church an hour from where we live. I stopped on the way home and ate twenty chicken nuggets with five containers of BBQ sauce before I came through the door to make sure I got some meat, because of the chance my wonderful wife wouldn't be cooking any. How do people survive if they don't eat meat? Better yet, how do people survive eating just fruits, vegetables and a few side dishes? In the last few years, I have learned a great deal about the importance of having a well-rounded and plant-based diet. Now, I am a vegetarian.

As we saw in the section about exercise, a proper diet works well only if it is consistent and sustainable. I am not trying to convince you of what you need to eat, but I will share what has worked well for me. I hope it encourages you in your health and fitness journey to reduce health-related stress in your life.

Do our dietary habits affect our stress levels?

The short answer is, yes. A wise man once told me, "Some people live to eat, and others eat to live." There is a lot of truth in that statement. Every day we wake up craving something. For some, the craving is physical exercise. For others, it may be prayer or meditation time. Yet, for others, it may be food. For my kids, it has always been food. The first thing they ask every morning when I see them is, "When can we eat?"

Important factors to consider in any diet are moderation, portion control and self-control. Here are a few rules I follow that help me control my diet:

1.   The 80% rule. Eat until you are 80% full. This involves practicing all three factors mentioned above. In our home, we decided to get rid of our biggest plates and now use medium sized plates. If we plan to put food on every inch of our plate, we should use smaller plates to help us with moderation and portion control. Self-control is seen in not making the trip for seconds! Eating until we are stuffed is not good for any of our internal systems. If we can control the amounts of food we eat and not stuff ourselves past 80%, there will be less pressure (stress) within our body and our digestive system functions more efficiently.

2.   Fast for half of every day. I do my best to have my last meal each night before 6:00 PM. I eat breakfast each morning between 7:00 and 8:00 AM so that I get at least twelve hours between eating. Most research shows this kind of fasting elevates metabolism and lowers cholesterol. I also try to fast for 24-48 hours every few months to detox. During these fasts I drink just water and sometimes a little coffee on the first day. From what I have read, 50% of

doctors/researchers report coffee in moderation (many say four cups a day) has proven to be beneficial for digestion and metabolism. Granted, you can find research to prove otherwise so I encourage you to use your own discretion on the coffee. Two cups a day is what is helpful for my digestion and well-being.

3.   Drink lots of water. Lots. It took me years to learn the value of hydration and I played sports most of my life. I thought I would weigh more if I consumed more water so I didn't drink as much as I should. The better hydrated your muscles are, the better they perform. At the very least, I drink a ½ oz of water per day for every pound of body weight, but I try to drink 1 oz per pound of body weight as often as I can, especially when I'm exercising. This is helpful to your joints as well as your muscles.

These three rules may not work for everyone, but they work well for me. Our appetites are not genetic. We get to choose the quality and quantity of what we eat. We have the power to train our bodies to crave certain types of food. For example, when I was growing up, I hated peas and nearly every kind of bean. Now, the biggest staples in my diet are bean burritos and chickpea salad. I have trained myself not to just tolerate healthy food, but to crave and enjoy it. It may take a little time, but you can do it!

Sadly, we have this knowledge as adults, but the majority don't take proper precautions to train their kids to crave healthy foods. We live in such a fast-paced society the cheap and easy way out is often what our kids eat. Fast food, microwave dinners, and so many other options are saturated with more preservatives than we can count or pronounce. It is no wonder immune systems are down and the percentage of kids who take medicine because of dietary needs continues to increase. My kids are fortunate to have a mother who makes sure their bodies get the proper nutrition to help protect them from food-related disease development. A rule of thumb in our house when looking at ingredients of our groceries is this: if we can't pronounce it, we don't buy it.

Why is being healthy important when it comes to stress? Disease attacks and destroys our body from the inside out and puts stress or pressure on the various systems of the body and demands they work harder than normal to fight off infection and illness. To prevent this from happening, we must understand the effects of malnutrition.

I have found the biggest factors in developing a plan for decreasing health-related stress are the same for both exercise and diet: consistency and sustainability. When we consider the specifics of how we plan to eat, we need to ask ourselves if our plan is sustainable. For example, if we plan to eat meat only and cut out nearly all carbs to lose weight, can we do this for the long term? Will this be beneficial to our bodies? Are the long-term effects as good as the short-term results? There are pros and cons to each diet that exists, so we must do our homework.

It is important to research the effects of whichever dietary plan we implement and then also decide if we will commit to it for the long haul. When I stopped eating meat, I challenged myself to do something that was sustainable. I was able to commit for the short term which was a good start. I didn't plan to be a vegetarian for the long haul, but the longer I live without eating meat, the better I feel. I did lose a few pounds, but that wasn't the reason for changing my eating habits. I'm not going to preach a sermon on vegetarianism, but I am amazed at how little people understand the benefits of a plant-based diet. Many people have asked me where I get protein if I don't get it from meat. I have to laugh a little when I ask, "where do animals get protein?" Animals get their protein from the grass, grains and vegetation they eat. A vegetarian is cutting out the middle man or animal and going straight to the source.

Just a few specifics on my diet are:

Bean burritos – Purple Cabbage, greens, onions, black beans, salsa, whole wheat tortilla.

Oatmeal – I eat a bowl of oatmeal at least twice a day. Every morning for breakfast and a small bowl as a night time snack after dinner. I put ½ cup of oats in a bowl along with 1 tablespoon of peanut butter (organic, no oils), 1 tablespoon of honey or creamed honey and a sprinkle of cinnamon. I add cashew milk before heating in the microwave for one minute.

I could eat these two items for any and every meal. Both are packed with nutrients (including protein) and the oatmeal always feels like dessert. It may sound boring to some, but I love it. We all need to find healthy food choices that we enjoy if we plan to make a lifestyle of healthy eating.

Prolonged or extreme dieting puts your body under stress, which increases cortisol production. As a result, your adrenal glands continue to release the stress-causing hormone cortisol 24/7, causing muscle loss and weight gain. For this reason, we must choose an eating lifestyle that is healthy and sustainable instead of dieting every few months and putting undue stress on our body that causes anxiety.

As I mentioned earlier, I fast for at least twelve hours every day.

"One of the newest weight loss recommendations is intermittent fasting, and it actually rebels against current research that tells you to eat when you're hungry and have six meals a day. Skipping your lunch break or going the entire day without any calories may not only be a weight loss recommendation, but also the trick to a longer life. Reducing calorie consumption 30 to 40 percent can extend a person's life span by a third or more, as many animal studies have shown, by making the brain resistant to toxins than cause cellular damage" (https://www.medicaldaily.com/how-3-meals-day-became-rule-and-why-we-should-be-eating-whenever-we-get-hungry-324892).

Excuse or license?

Before we look at how T.R.I.A.L.S. can help us reduce health related anxiety, I want to mention again how important genetics are when we consider our health-related goals. Regardless of having "good genes" or "bad genes," we can't use our genetics as a license to eat whatever we want or an excuse to not attempt a healthier life style. Unfortunately, some of us are born with diseases we cannot control which limit the way we can exercise and certain foods we can eat. I encourage you to have a positive outlook and understand there are still enjoyable ways to eat and exercise. Eat to live, don't live to eat and focus on the blessing of life. For those who don't have dietary and exercise restrictions, I encourage you to eat to live as well. It took me a long time to learn this lesson. I always felt good, and I could eat whatever I wanted. Now, I eat foods that help prevent disease in my body and I don't feel good, I feel great! More importantly, I don't have anxiety because of my diet and exercise.

I love what Paul says in 1 Corinthians 9:23 – 27. "*I do all things for the sake of the gospel, so that I may become a fellow partaker of it. Do you not know that those who run in a race all run, but only one receives the prize? Run in such a way that you may win. Everyone who competes in the games exercises self-control in all things. They then do it to receive a perishable wreath, but we an imperishable.* ²⁶ *Therefore, I run in such a way, as not without aim; I box in such a way, as not beating the air; but I discipline my body and make it my slave, so that, after I have preached to others, I myself will not be disqualified.*"

Look at verse 25, *"everyone who competes in the games exercises self-control in all things."* This is the key to diet and exercise. Self-control. It may not always be easy, but it is always worth it. Are we willing to discipline our bodies, making them our slave? Why should we? Why is physical health so important? God has a plan for us and our lives. If we use self-control to take care of the physical body God has given us, we can potentially live longer, more enjoyable lives reaping the benefits of the spiritual blessings and will of God for our lives here on this earth. It's not just about quantity of years lived but quality of years lived.

Regardless of which workout routine and diet you decide to embrace, if you go through T.R.I.A.L.S., you learn to eliminate stress and live a healthy lifestyle. When it comes to physical fitness and diet, the application of T.R.I.A.L.S. provides the same benefits.

Transparency – When you start your journey to healthier living and eating, there can be no secrets. This does not mean splurging on occasion is forbidden. It also doesn't mean you must splurge. However, there is a huge difference in a cheat meal and a cheat day and a cheat weekend and a … you get the point. My suggestion is to get an accountability partner. Nearly every time I fast for one or two days, I have a friend who fasts with me, so we can check in and challenge each other. Misery loves company, and when we challenge ourselves to do something difficult, an accountability partner is very helpful.

Responsibility – We cannot change our past, so we must accept our present circumstances if we want to move forward in our journey to reduce stress by living a healthier lifestyle. If we start where we are, use what we have and do what we can, we can assemble a sustainable and attainable plan. We must be diligent when putting our plan into practice. Responsibility is significant in many ways. For example, if we plan to exercise every morning at 5:00 AM, we need to set our alarm for the appropriate time to make this happen. If we plan to stop eating junk food, we need to get rid of the junk food in our house and avoid going to places where we are tempted to eat something that isn't healthy. In our house, we don't buy chips and junk food. This makes it easier to avoid unhealthy food. At times, being responsible requires sacrifice. Accept the challenge and embrace the results!

Intentionality – No one ever became healthier on accident. People don't get healthy from eating unhealthy foods and not exercising. Exercising and eating healthy are intentional decisions. When we find ourselves tempted to be lazy and eat junk food, we need a plan that reminds us of our goals. An effective way to do this is to place notes in strategic locations, like in the kitchen, by your shoes, and places you go often.

Present moment awareness is essential to overcoming food temptations. At meal times, I suggest taking five deep breaths before you start eating. Learn to chew more and put the utensil down between bites. Writing down goals and plans is a great start to intentional and healthy living.

Appreciation – Self-appreciation is a huge part of healthy living. When we are willing to take care of our own mind and body, we need to show ourselves gratitude. Take a walk, excursion, get a massage, download some new music, or spend time practicing your favorite hobby. Write a book! That's what I did. Learning to appreciate and reward ourselves can be of great encouragement and motivation in our journey to reduce stress and feel better.

Limits – With diet and exercise, we must know our limits, or we can find ourselves in awkward and difficult situations. Remember the 80% rule when eating. When we take our first deep breath toward the end of a meal, that is a sign we should have stopped sooner. Pushing our limits while eating is not helpful in relieving stress; it does the opposite. With exercising, pushing our limits often leads to injury. We must listen to our bodies and back off when our limits are in sight, not after we pass them.

Simplify – There are many ways to simplify what we eat and how we exercise. If you must have dessert every day, one way you can simplify is to pick a day not to eat dessert or create a dessert that is healthy. I feel I eat dessert every day because oatmeal is my favorite thing to eat. In case you need the reminder…1/2 cup of oats, tablespoon of peanut butter, little cinnamon, tablespoon of honey and milk of your choice (I use cashew milk). One minute in the microwave, mix well and enjoy!

An easy way to simplify your exercise routine is to find three or four exercises that help each part of the body instead of picking ten exercises for each workout routine. Part of simplifying may mean committing to five or ten minutes a day instead of an hour. An hour can be unachievable many times, but we can reduce that to five or ten minutes. The simple daily work out will be much more effective than the hour we can't commit to on most days. Unless you plan to train for a physique competition or body-building event, having five exercises for each muscle group may be overkill. We must listen to our body when we eat and when we exercise.

Motivation: Regardless of your physical health, sit down and make some goals. These should include dietary goals and exercise goals. Share your goal with someone who will allow you to check in and make sure you stay on task. Start where you are, use what you have, and do what you can. If you can't think of a single goal, start with a commitment to a five-minute workout every day, no negotiating. Even if it means walking the hallway for five minutes, do something. You can do it!

Advice: Don't compare your health to others. Everyone has different genetics and their routines may be lifelong or something they just started. You do you.

Prayer: Thank you, Lord, for my health. Help me to believe I have the power to develop self-control so that I can preserve the body you have given me and work in your service for many years to come. May I always look to you for strength and motivation as I try to serve others. Amen.

Chapter 8 - Faith and Anxiety

By now, you have probably eliminated anxiety in your life that comes from your job, your finances, raising your kids and your marriage. I can only imagine you have decided to work out several times a week and are now a vegetarian. The only thing left to do now is figure out if anxiety exists in your life because of your faith or religious convictions and how you can eliminate this stress as well.

Is being physically healthy easy? For some, it is. In our home, it is not a challenge because we have created a lifestyle of exercise and eating healthy foods. However, for many people in the world, it can be a great challenge.

What about our spiritual health? Is being spiritually healthy easy? For those who have grown up in a Christian home, the answer to the question may be positive. However, I have visited with many people who grew up in a loving, Christian family who have anxiety because of their faith. For the unchurched, spiritual health may not even be on the radar.

What is faith? Where does it come from? Where did your faith come from? When I was growing up, my dad was a preacher. I had a great example of what being faithful is all about. I learned a lot about the Bible and spiritual goals I should set for myself on a daily basis. However, a good portion of "my faith" was a result of my parents' faith. I was baptized when I was 17 years old and did my best to put God first in my life.

It wasn't until I was a few years into college that I began to develop my own faith. In high school, I put 100% confidence in what my parents taught me and still believe they did everything they could to encourage me to study and make my faith my own. However, it wasn't until I was on my own that I really developed the convictions I needed to grow in my personal faith. Many topics I didn't study in high school that I studied in college began to help me develop better study habits and deeper convictions.

Perhaps your faith is the result of your parents or a spouse, co-worker, friend, children, or another relationship important in your life. Regardless of the factors that have shaped what you believe, it is your belief. This past year, I have studied with more atheists than I can remember. I've been laughed at for "believing in something I can't see." When I respond to their laughter by asking them if they believe in air or gravity, it allows us to discuss believing in the effects or the evidence of things we don't see. What we believe is important. However, the more important aspect of your spiritual life is your faithfulness. On the day of judgment, you will give an account for you and you alone. I can't be held accountable for what someone else says or does. I will be judged on my life. Faithfulness is important.

I recently sat down with my dad as he was preparing to teach through the book of Hebrews and he pointed out that the word translated faith has much more to do with how you live, not what you believe. Belief is important. The Bible is important. However, being faithful to the commitment we make when agree for Jesus to be Lord of our life is much more important.

Do we worry about our spiritual well-being? Does it cause us anxiety? Several questions or feelings we have plague us when it comes to why anxiety builds up in our life. For example, I don't know enough about the Bible. I'm not doing enough. I can't be perfect. Other people do more than I. God can't forgive me for what I've done. The list goes on. I have studied with a couple for over two years about faith and salvation. They can recite what the Bible teaches about how we become a Christian, but they still are not ready to make the commitment. They tell me they still need to know more.

When I was in Mexico studying Spanish, the group I was with had the opportunity to help a local church with different projects during the week and each evening a few of us would go to one of the member's house for a Bible study. On one occasion, two from our group were preparing to go the Bible study, but they didn't want to go. I remember so well when they asked my teacher if they had to go. They said, "Haven't we done enough?" I'll never forget how he responded. He said, "You look at the man on the cross and ask Him if you have done enough." Ouch. Guess who decided to go to the study?

It doesn't matter how much we do or don't do. God expects us to have a better attitude. Paul says, "Have this same mindset in you that was also in Christ Jesus." Can we do enough? No. Our attitude needs to be "how can I do more?" How can I do more to please the God who has given me all things? How can I grow in my faithfulness when I have so many doubts and fears?

It is important to understand Satan has a powerful arsenal and he is relentless when it comes to destroying our faithfulness to God. He never stops. He wants to hurt us. The three most powerful tools he uses against us are fear, doubt, and pride. They all do something different. Fear cripples us. Fear of the unknown causes us not to do anything at all. It doesn't matter how great or small the task; when we are afraid to put our faith on the line because of the unknown outcome, fear causes us to not do anything at all. Doubt causes us to hesitate. Hesitation causes us to miss opportunities or it may cause us to make mistakes because we don't put our full trust in God to accomplish His will in our lives.

On the other end of this spectrum, when we overcome doubt and fear and we tackle the spiritual battle with all we have, the temptation of pride comes along. It makes us think we can do it on our own. I don't think I have to mention what comes before a great fall. When we begin to pat our own back because of things we have accomplished, we better look out. The slope is slippery.

We also need to understand God has tools as well. Philippians 2 explains the attitude of Jesus and the tools He used and make available to us. Humility and confidence are weapons that help us overcome doubt, fear and pride. Humility allows us to understand we need help. Regardless of the task in front of us, we need to approach it with humility. In the book of Luke, Jesus tells a parable about two men that go to the temple to pray. Like the Pharisees, one of these men was arrogant, haughty and thought well of himself. The other was humble and contrite of heart. Which of these two men was justified? Which one was received by God? The humble man! We need to be humble when it comes to our faithfulness. There may be great spiritual things accomplished in our lives. God is the only one who deserves praise and glory. Period. This is what confidence is all about; knowing God is the one in control and it is He who works in our lives for His purpose and good will.

When we understand it is God working, it takes the stress off our plate and allows us to eliminate anxiety when it comes to working for God in His kingdom. Plant the seed. God will do the rest. Plant the seed.

Often at the end of sermons, we hear the question, "if you were to die tonight, are you 100% certain you would go to heaven?" Then, we hear the invitation. We may think there are only two times a week we can be sure of our relationship with God. I disagree. I would encourage you right now to ask yourself this question. If the answer is "No, I'm not sure," I don't know how you sleep at night. I mean this with all sincerity of heart. How do you sleep at night? God wants you to have confidence. He wants you to know without a doubt your eternity is secured with Him!

I have studied with people who have told me they would not go to heaven if they died. When I ask them, "Why not make your life right with God right now?" they responded, "in the future." They tell me they know what they need to do, but they want to wait. I can't understand. If you are not 100% in your faithfulness you would go to heaven if you died right now, you need to talk to someone. Don't finish this chapter without knowing the certainty of your salvation. If you want to talk to me, my email address is turnerc23@yahoo.com and you can write me any time. I am here for you. I will respond.

God gives us clear instructions. In Acts 2:38, Peter responds to people who asked about what they needed to do to remove the sin problem in their life. They asked, "*What do we need to do to be saved?*" Peter said, "*Repent and be baptized, every one of you in the name of Jesus Christ for the remission of your sins.*" Remission, forgiveness, salvation. This is what we need. It's more than just repenting and being baptized. That's just the beginning. It's knowing that repentance is not a one-time decision, but a lifelong process of growing and changing as we seek to improve our walk with God. It's about walking in the light as Jesus is in the light. It's leaning on God's people and building relationships with people who will challenge us to do better and encourage us in our faithfulness.

In John 12:42 – 43, we read, "*Yet at the same time, many among the leaders believed in Him. But because of the Pharisees, they would not openly acknowledge their faith for fear they would be put out of the synagogue; for they loved human praise more than praise from God.*"

Does that ever cause us to stutter or stop? Does human praise appeal to us? Do we hesitate to do a good thing because we are afraid of what someone else might think of us? I love this text in John 12. The last part is my favorite. When he says, "*for they loved human praise more than the praise of God.*" Do you know what that implies? We are praiseworthy by our creator when we acknowledge Him before other people! Can you imagine God being thankful for us? Do you remember Job? God asks Satan, "Have you considered my servant Job?" Can we put our name in the blank? Have you considered my servant _____? God praises us when we do right, even if we can't see it. That's what He gives us.

In Luke 12:8, Luke says, "*I tell you, whoever publicly acknowledges me before others, the Son of man will also acknowledge before the angels of God.*"

How do we do this? How do we publicly acknowledge God? I don't believe we are to stand on street corners or in the store parking lot with a speaker system and shout, "Repent for the kingdom of heaven is at hand!" I haven't seen much success or any success from people who take this approach. Have you ever walked up to those who do this because you wanted to study with them? Me either.

One of my suggestions is to invite God into conversations. When someone asks us how we are, why not respond with "I'm good, thanks be to God. He has provided me everything I need." If we aren't doing so great, why not respond with, "I'm not doing too well because _____, but God is still good. He loves me and gave His Son for me." Acknowledging our blessings come from God is a good thing. Why not fill our conversations with these good things as opposed to the weather, sports, small talk that do not help people come to know our God? I'm not saying visiting about life and culture with others is bad. I am saying we should always look for teachable moments and introducing God into our conversations.

1st Peter 2:1 – 2 says, "*Therefore, laying aside all malice, all deceit, hypocrisy, envy, and all evil speaking, as newborn babes, desire the pure milk of the word, that you may grow thereby, if indeed you have tasted that the Lord is gracious."*

Do we want to grow in our faithfulness? Part of spiritual growth is spiritual nutrition. We are to crave the pure milk of the word. We live in a time in which we can freely obtain a Bible in just about any language and translation we want. There are more free online resources for downloading tools to help us understand scripture than ever before. Can you imagine how this would have impacted the church 1,000 years ago? 100 years ago? Shame on us if we don't take advantage of what technology makes available to us!

In the parenting chapter, I shared with you my kids' answer when I asked them what I could do better as a parent. Time. They wanted my time. If we are going to use the same mindset, "my faith would be stronger if _____", how would we respond? I posted this question on Facebook and got several responses. One of them was, "I gave FULL control instead of trying to do certain things myself or my way." Another responded, "I spent more time with Christians instead of worldly people/influences." The last two responses really hit home for me and I believe many others as well. They were, "If I spent less time worrying about other people and what they think of me" and "If I spent more time alone with God."

Is this us? Have we run out of time? Do we not have enough time left at the end of the day to spend with God and His people? How do we fill our day? Most things that help us grow spiritually are challenging. They are challenging because they force us to change. If we spend more time with other Christians, we may have to change our schedule. We may have to change the way we look at someone. We may have to put ourselves aside and put others first.

In every aspect of life, if we are going to grow, we must change. How many of us want to be told we are doing something wrong? How many of us want to hear, "What you're doing isn't wrong, but there is a better way to do it." None of us. One of the hardest things for any of us to do is admit we aren't doing something right or in the best way. Why? Pride! What if we learn to use God's tools of humility and confidence so we can grow?

What are we looking for in our faith and faithfulness? Is there something specific we are hoping to get out of doing that we believe God expects from us? Do we have a checklist? Are we looking to just do enough? What does enough look like for you? When we looked at finances, I shared a definition of enough given in a Bible class I attended on finances. The teacher said the definition of enough was "Just a little bit more." What if we applied this definition to our faithfulness?

What if our attitude was, I'll be content with my faithfulness when I do just a little bit more for the kingdom. If we will do this, we will never stop doing for God. That's what God expects of us. Don't be merely hearers, but doers. We were created for selfless action.

If someone were to ask you, "Which is more difficult: being a Christian or being evangelistic in your community?" How would you respond? Can we be a Christian and not be evangelistic? I can't be a Christian unless I am going to tell other people about Jesus, can I? The command is in the Bible. This is our reference for most of what we do and don't do. Why do you attend church services? The Bible says to. Why aren't you involved in drinking, lying, adultery, etc. The Bible says not to. There is plenty more to Christianity than avoiding evil. We are commanded to be proactive in our Christianity.

Why is it so difficult for us to evangelize? Do we really believe what our faith says we believe? Do we set spiritual goals? Every year, my wife and I sit down and make goals for every area of our life, including our spiritual life. When we challenge ourselves spiritually, we ask ourselves about growing in our faithfulness. What are some things we can commit to action in our lives to be faithful to our commitment to growing in Christ? How can we be more evangelistic? What if we all committed to doing whatever it takes to reach one person with the good news of Jesus? I'm not just talking about inviting someone to church services. What if we invited them into our home and showed them Jesus is as much a part of our family and home life as He is when we are together with His people on Sunday? What if we didn't have to invite people to come to Bible class or a time of edification with the church because they asked us first, "Where do you attend?" or "What church do you belong to?" The church could grow at astronomical rates if we would commit to spiritual goals and evangelism as we do other areas in our life.

God has given us all different talents and abilities. We don't have to know every book, chapter and verse to get to heaven or to help others get to heaven. Your gift may not be remembering scriptures. That doesn't mean you shouldn't study, but it means you shouldn't put the pressure and stress on yourself to have the entire Bible memorized. If the future of the church hinged on my ability to lead singing, we would all be in trouble. That isn't my talent, not by a long shot. That doesn't mean I shouldn't sing, but rather maybe I shouldn't be the song leader. I should look for the talents God has given me and use them for His kingdom.

To the leaders in the church, I give you the task of knowing your congregation well enough that you can give opportunities to those with different talents to use them to help the church in areas they are able.

To the workers in the church, I give you the task of sharing your talents with others. If you are a great song leader, but you don't tell anyone, it is going to be difficult to take advantage of that gift. If you are a technology guru, but you don't tell anyone, it will be difficult to get involved if no one knows you are good with technology. Communicate well and then be a doer.

Self-reflection is important. In 2 Corinthians 10:12, Paul says, *"For we are not bold to class or compare ourselves with some of those who commend themselves; but when they measure themselves by themselves and compare themselves with themselves, they are without understanding."* What in the world does this have to do with my faith? Some things we can do to help ourselves in our faithfulness, but some things we can do that will not help us. In fact, some things we can do will hurt us in our spiritual growth.

We have looked several times at comparative living. We have looked at how we have a desire to be normal. I want to be a normal husband. I want to be a normal employee. I want to have normal clothes and drive a normal car that everyone will think is okay. I want my kids to be normal. I want to be a normal Christian. I just want to come to church to pray, give, sing, listen to a sermon, take the Lord's supper and then go home. Just let me be normal. I have encouraged us all, several times, to rid our vocabulary of the word "normal." Life is not about being normal; it's about being like Jesus. He was not normal. He was so different than everyone else. When we begin to compare ourselves to other people in any area of life, we do one of two things:

1. We will think: I am not doing nearly enough. This person over here is doing A, B, C, D, and E, and I'm only doing A. This will cause us to have doubt. This will cause us to take the focus off what we need to do because we are so concerned about what others are doing.

2. We will think: This person over here isn't hardly doing anything. Look at me, I'm doing A and B, and they are only doing A.

Comparing ourselves to others will never be helpful in our spiritual growth and will most certainly cause us stress and anxiety as we try to keep up or puff ourselves up based on the amount we are doing or what someone else is not doing.

> *Comparing ourselves to others will never be helpful in our spiritual growth*

We must learn to acknowledge our gifts and then put them to use. If you go to a marina to get a job on a boat and they ask you, "Do you know anything about boats?" and you answer "No", you aren't likely to get a job. If you go to a professional basketball tryout, but you don't know how to dribble a basketball, the tryout will not go well. If you are interested in getting involved in ministry, you need to know what you are good at. Knowing your gift or gifts is as important as putting them to use.

> *"As leaders, it is never our responsibility to fill anyone else's cup. Our responsibility is to empty ours." – Andy Stanley*

For me, it was speaking Spanish. I don't have many talents, but I do speak Spanish. It took me eight years of attending at our congregation before I put my abilities to speak Spanish into a local evangelistic effort. Shame on me for waiting so long! You have an ability to do something. Get involved! The greatest thing you can do to increase your faithfulness is serve other people. Take the focus off you. That's the benefit of being involved in ministry. It's not what I get out of it, but how I can help someone else. In his book *Deep and Wide,* Andy Stanley says, "As leaders, it is never our responsibility to fill anyone else's cup. Our responsibility is to empty ours" (Stanley, p.11).

One of the other problems we run into is judging the faithfulness of others. If someone says, "He or she is a faithful Christian," what is the first thing that comes to our mind? They never miss a service. They are here every time the doors are open! Isn't this the picture we create? I know lots of congregations that don't meet on Wednesday night or Sunday night. Can they still be faithful Christians? I don't recall seeing a command to judge others, but many times we are commanded to love others, especially Christians. Instead of judging or condemning folks who don't make it every time the doors are open, let's show them an extra measure of love and encouragement.

I'm not saying we should skip services. I love being around my brothers and sisters in Christ. Sunday is my favorite day of the week. My family is at the building from 9:00 AM until 3:30 or 4:00 PM every Sunday. It's exhausting! Sunday nights are great because we get to sit down, relax and reflect on how God was able to work through us. I've never had a problem sleeping on Sunday nights!

My faithfulness has grown because of the service God has blessed us to participate in while reaching out to the Hispanics in our area. Every time they take a break in their schedule to come edify us with their presence, it is glorifying to God and uplifting to me. Every time there is a need in the group and we can help meet that need, there is a renewed sense of energy and love that is unexplainable. There is something to helping others that helps ourselves.

Throughout the Old Testament, God constantly reminded His faithful leaders of one important fact. He was with them. When Joshua was charged with the task of leading the Israelites after Moses died, God repeatedly told him, *"Be strong and courageous and do not be afraid. I will be with you."* As Christians, we have the same promise from Jesus right before He left the earth. He tells us He will be with us until the very end, according to Matthew 28.

God is with you. When you feel your faithfulness begin to waiver, there is no greater place to turn than to your heavenly Father. There is nowhere else He wants you to turn as well. Perhaps that is why Paul says, *"Be anxious for nothing but in everything with prayer."* Being faithful requires us to have faith in something we may not be able to physically see. This is part of the journey for a Christian. Trust God is there for you.

Knowing and trusting God is with us every step of the way should eliminate anxiety from our faithfulness to Him. If we feel we haven't helped a single soul come to Jesus, my suggestion is for us to treat our faith like a seed. We must plant it in the right places. The best place for me to plant may not be the best place for you to plant. We all have a group that does not listen to us and a group that does. Paul was called to preach to one group because of his background and Peter was called to preach to another group. Your co-workers and friends are people I may never meet, and I'm connected to people you may never meet. Let's plant where we are.

We must also water with encouragement and love as we try to help others see Jesus through our words and actions. The most important aspect of treating our faith like a seed is letting God provide the increase. That is what He has asked us to do. I'm still studying with people that have not accepted Jesus as their Savior. It's been nearly three years. Is it my fault? Why won't they obey? Can you imagine how much anxiety and stress I would have if I felt it was my responsibility to provide increase? My job is to plant, and that's what I continue to do. When they are convicted enough to obey, God will provide the increase and God will receive the glory. If we are stressed because we wait to receive glory for others coming to Jesus, we have missed the point of evangelism completely. God provides the increase, and if He uses you or me along the way, praise God for that opportunity.

I love gardening. I also love the great parallel that exists between gardening and evangelism. Our garden this year has produced two massive watermelons, over thirty giant cucumbers, forty jalapeños, several tomatoes and more leafy greens than I can count. Why? Is it because I'm a miracle-working gardener? No, it is because God is amazing and can use someone as simple minded as me to put a seed in the ground and put water on it from time to time. Would anything grow without me putting seed in the ground? No. I had to do something. Evangelism works the same way. If we don't plant the seed, people may never have the opportunity to meet Jesus. We must do our part. He will use us if we let Him.

At the end of each one of these chapters on anxiety, we have looked at how the T.R.I.A.L.S. method can help us decrease stress and eliminate anxiety in our life. It works in the same capacity with our faith. Are we willing to be vulnerable or would we rather live with anxiety? Let's choose peace. Dive in to T.R.I.A.L.S. and see how anxiety can be eliminated for you.

Transparency: Often times we live in denial when it comes to some aspects of our faith. We must be open and honest with ourselves and our relationship with God. We cannot deny that Satan is real and that he works every day to tempt us and create doubt, fear, and pride. Check in with yourself and see where you can improve if you have doubts or fears within your daily walk. Trust Jesus to help you as you set and achieve your spiritual goals.

Responsibility: If there are sins you have committed in the past and you still suffer with the consequences, accept those consequences and take responsibility for them. Accept those consequences and be responsible for things from your past.

That doesn't mean to dwell on them but make the best choices possible starting today. Focus on the present moment the responsibilities you have in your faithfulness. Figure out your talents and start using them for kingdom growth.

Intentionality: Spiritual growth will not happen by accident. You must choose it. Don't wait for faithfulness to happen. Make faithfulness happen. Every choice we make must be with intention and the purpose of growing in our relationship with God and His people. Think first, then act. Be proactive, and you won't have to worry about being reactive.

Appreciation: When you work hard to be transparent, responsible, and intentional, God will reward your efforts. Take time to appreciate yourself for the work you do. If your spouse shares your faith, appreciate him or her for it. If your spouse shares in your ministry, show him or her gratitude. We can't make it on our own!

Limits: There are two areas in which we need to know our limits. The first is with temptation. If you know areas in life that tempt you, avoid them. Avoid them! Do not push the limits of your temptations. This will never help you. Replace tempting situations with positive, encouraging people or places. Temptation = desire plus opportunity. If we eliminate the desire or avoid the opportunity, we eliminate temptation.

The second area deals with the load you carry as a servant. At times you may feel your limits are being pushed regarding what you can offer. When we have the opportunity to serve but don't have the time or energy, we must learn it is okay to say, "No, thank you" or "I'm sorry, but I can't right now." I love to teach and preach, but my load is full right now. I'm at my limit. Every time I say "yes" to someone or something, I am saying "no" to something or someone else. Have priorities and stick to them. Know your limits. Don't push them.

Simplify: When our limits are pushed and anxiety begins to creep in, we must learn to simplify. This may require delegating spiritual opportunities and appointments to others who are willing to help us so we don't become overwhelmed. It is okay to simplify so that we don't burn out. Simplifying can also be a great way to do team building exercises and get more people involved in service. Use the resources you have.

Motivation: Challenge yourself this week to add one item of service to your faith. It may be something you do to serve others or to serve your own faith. Make a commitment to increase the time you spend serving God's people (this includes serving yourself!). If you are currently overwhelmed, the challenge for you is to simplify. Find a way to allow someone to help you with a current responsibility. Asking for help is tough, but it is worth it.

Advice: Ask someone for help. Even if you don't need help with what you are working on, ask for it anyway. Put pride aside and allow someone to help you. Work on building relationships in the kingdom.

Prayer: Thank you, Lord, for creating me to be me. Help me to always take advantage of opportunities to serve You and serve your people. Help me to focus on the spiritual more than the physical. When I am overwhelmed, help me to feel the peace You desire me to have because of Your Son and what He did for me. Amen.

Chapter 9 – Grief and Anxiety

Before you get too deep into this chapter, please know the content is not intended to help you if you are in the middle of tragedy. If you are experiencing intense grief right now, I am sorry your current circumstances are not ideal. If you would like prayers, email me and I promise to pray for you in the moment I receive it. I will do this.

As I share some of life's challenges we have faced in our home, you will see life is different for all of us. **Warning:** I have not experienced any extreme losses or tragedies. I'm not an expert on going through difficult times. You may have experienced similar struggles as our family or your life may have been or currently is difficult. My aim is to focus on prevention. The T.R.I.A.L.S. method is not something I created to solve every problem related to anxiety. It is a lifestyle I have lived for over a decade and it has served me well. When you apply these principles to life, your perception of grief changes and you learn to see through a lens that allows you to let go of how others expect you to act.

As in previous chapters, it is necessary to mention at the beginning how important it is not to use the word "normal" when we grieve or when others grieve. Grief is common to everyone in the sense that we all experience it, but we all grieve in different ways. If we aim to be like someone, it should be Jesus. Isaiah 53:3 says, *"He was despised, and rejected of men; Man of sorrows, and acquainted with grief: and as one from whom men hide their face he was despised; and we esteemed him not."* When we read through the New Testament, we see Jesus was a man who knew grief. He had friends who died. He had friends who betrayed Him and lost complete faith in Him as a friend, mentor, and master. His perspective was constant as He served others through His grief.

There is no standard for grief, but there is for anxiety. Grief is not always our choice, but anxiety is. Comparing how we feel or react during tragedy to how others feel or react is never

> *There is no standard for grief, but there is for anxiety.*

beneficial when it comes to avoiding anxiety. Trying to be like others can sometimes cause us more anxiety when we are grieving than the trial we are facing.

I'm not a big emotions kind of person. That's okay, I don't have to be. If I were to win a million dollars, I would be excited, but you wouldn't hear me screaming at the top of my lungs. At the same time, when I experience loss, I don't hide in a cave for a year or walk around with my head down for months as though my life is over. You may have big emotions and that's okay. As with all the other areas we study on anxiety, the key is self-control. When we allow others to determine how we should respond to a difficult situation, stress and potential anxiety are going to be the result.

The Two Causes of Anxiety related to Grief

Before we delve into the two causes of grief-related anxiety, we must define four words related to this topic: Grief, sad, sympathy and empathy. All the definitions come from Merriam-Webster's online dictionary. Grief is defined as "deep and poignant distress caused by or as if by bereavement." Sad is defined as "affected with or expressive of grief or unhappiness." Sympathy is defined as "an affinity, association, or relationship between persons or things wherein whatever affects one similarly affects the other." Empathy is defined as "the action of understanding, being aware of, being sensitive to, and vicariously experiencing the feelings, thoughts, and experience of another of either the past or present without having the feelings, thoughts and experience fully communicated in an objectively explicit manner" (www.merriam-webster.com).

When others experience grief, they will often be sad. We may empathize or sympathize with them. At times, sympathy is exactly what others need while grieving. Some prefer to grieve by themselves. Many years ago, before I was born, a friend of mine lost her father. She didn't want anyone close to her. She didn't want to talk to her husband or her friends. That's okay. Understanding how we need and want to grieve is important in helping us avoid anxiety, which is often the result of grief we are unprepared to experience.

What if?

The first cause of anxiety related to grief is something that doesn't happen. Countless events never take place and cause anxiety. Years ago, our oldest daughter developed a nodule in her throat. It started very small and we assumed it was nothing. A month later, it increased to the size of a marble, and we decided to see an ear, nose and throat doctor. He gave us a few options of what he thought it might be, but he gave us nothing definitive. He recommended us to see a surgeon to drain the mass to see what it was. After draining the cyst, they told us two things: 1. They still weren't sure what it was. 2. It shouldn't come back.

As you can imagine, we were less than thrilled with this information. Can you imagine the thoughts going through our minds? Let me help you out. The "c" word. We were afraid our little girl had cancer. The appointments, life span, quality of life, and help we would need are just a few of the struggles that began to creep into our minds and there wasn't a diagnosis. There wasn't even a suggestion of cancer, but the uncertainty filled us with dread. We were left with, what if? For a time, we lived in an imaginary world in which she did have cancer and real-life anxiety reared its head into our home.

We were thankful it *shouldn't* come back, but it did. This time, it was the size of a golf ball and we were sent to New Orleans to see a specialist. By the time we saw the specialist, it wasn't any bigger and he told us the MRI showed it was a thyroglossal duct cyst, which could be removed surgically. We returned home, and scheduled surgery to remove the cyst. After successful surgery, thankfully, it hasn't returned.

This whole process was several months long, and the world kept spinning while we dealt with our potential life-changing situation. Did you catch the key word? Potential. We lived every day in doubt and wonder of what could have happened. We also had to explain all of this to a little girl who wanted to play as if nothing was wrong. I felt like I needed to wrap her in a bubble so nothing bad would happen to her, and it was exhausting.

If you look online, you will find a variety of people with an opinion of the exact percentage of things we worry about that never happen, but the bottom line is this: We worry about a lot of stuff that doesn't happen. The question is, why? Fear of the unknown? Fear of change? Fear of _____? Fear causes anxiety. It doesn't have to, but it does for many of us.

It happened, now what?

The second cause of anxiety related to grief is what does happen. Life presents us with situations every day and we become anxious. Many of these circumstances are outside our control. A few years ago, my grandfather passed on as the result of a heart attack. It was difficult for our whole family. I was strong. I held my emotions inside because many needed me to be stable at the time. At the graveside, while trying to say a few words, I completely lost it. The emotions began to come out. The grief I was holding onto was stronger than my will to hide the emotion. I cannot understate enough; grieving is not wrong. In fact, there are times we need to grieve. It is okay to be emotional.

The hard lesson to learn is how not to allow grief to become anxiety. What is our response to grief? Does it consume us? Does it create inner turmoil that shuts us down to the point we don't want to leave the house or see anyone? I won't suggest how to deal with your grief, especially if you are in the middle of a tragedy. I want you to keep reading. I will offer some tools and resources to help prepare yourself for the next time grief comes your way.

Why do we experience grief? This question causes many to doubt the existence of God. How could an all-loving God allow anyone, especially Christians, to experience suffering and tribulation? "Allow" doesn't mean "force." Laws are placed in effect to keep us safe. Gravity keeps us grounded unless we choose to fly in a plane or climb a ladder. Understanding the consequences of ignoring gravity and jumping from a high area with no safety precautions is important if we want to avoid physical pain. We must be prepared to avoid injury. Preparation is key to avoiding most forms of physical pain. It is also key to avoiding most forms of emotional pain, such as grief.

When I was twelve, my grandmother told me I was going to make a fine gospel preacher when I was older. I smiled and told her I loved that Grandpa and dad were preachers, but "it isn't for me." I will remember this conversation for the rest of my life. One of the reasons I didn't want to preach full-time was because I didn't want to perform weddings and funerals. I didn't want to deal with emotional people, whether they were happy or sad. Doesn't that sound terrible? Twenty-three years later, I am not only a full-time minister for a Spanish congregation, I do it voluntarily. I wouldn't have it any other way.

I have also taught for many years in several congregations around our area and have developed great relationships with many. As a result, I get asked to do weddings and funerals. Several years ago, a good friend of mine who was 82 asked me if I would preach his funeral. He lived nine hours away. I told him, "As long as you don't plan to die, I will do it." Less than a year later, I received a call from his wife on a Sunday morning. I knew instantly what happened. I was scheduled to teach a seminar in Costa Rica the following week, but the funeral took place a few days before my trip and I was able to attend. On my way home, I was pulled over for speeding. It was unintentional. I was in a construction zone and didn't know. I did my best to explain to the officer why I was in town and I didn't realize it was a construction zone. She didn't care about my grief. She wrote the ticket. There are times when others won't sympathize with us. That's okay, they don't have to. I decided not to preach any more funerals.

Two years later, I was asked to preach the funeral for another friend. He was twenty-one years old. Declining was not something I was prepared to do to his family, so I said I would speak at the funeral. There was a big difference in emotions between preaching the funeral of an eighty-two year old and a twenty-one-year-old. These two individuals had lived completely different lives. One hadn't lived very long at all.

How do you cope with grief when you lose a spouse or a child? To be honest, I'm not sure because I've never lost a parent or a child. It's beyond difficult to feel you have helped someone through these kinds of trials. When others are grieving, it's not about you, it's about them. How helpful you feel you were is irrelevant. I try not to consider my own feelings at all when others are grieving unless we are grieving for the same thing. When offering support to others, it needs to be all about them. Before I share my approach to helping

127

others who are suffering, I want to share what I know isn't helpful. Thankfully, these are lessons I have learned from others and not my own experiences.

Even if you have experienced a similar tragedy to a friend who is currently suffering, the words, "I know what you are going through" are never helpful. Never. Don't use them. Saying, "God is in control. You just need to pray" is not always comforting, even if it's true. More times than not, physical presence and silence are more helpful than anything else. Short visits are better than long visits, unless you are asked to stay. It will be obvious if the grieving family or friend wants you to stay. Do what they need you to do, not what you need.

As the person responsible for speaking during the time of suffering for my friends, my nerves tried to get the best of me. I love public speaking, but I do not love funerals. I prepare well for sermons and classes, but I spend a little extra time preparing for grieving occasions. I shared several personal stories during both funerals. I consulted the Bible for most of what I said. In my attempt to relate emotions and grief to these families, I shared lessons I learned from a study through the book of Job. He knew grief as much as anyone and because of his relationship with God, he was prepared for anything life presented to him.

Job was a righteous man and the wealthiest of his time. Read Job chapter 1 and see the abundance of his possessions. Further investigation shows he not only lost a mass of wealth, but he also lost ten children and his health. The remnant of a support system he had left advised him to curse God and die. This is misery. This is grief. No doubt, he was sad. What keeps someone going when trials of the greatest magnitude flood their world? Faith. Friends. Family. Unfortunately, Job lost his family. His friends were useless to him. His faithfulness to God, unwavering. Job responded as I hope I would have. If I ever face calamity as he did, I hope my response would be, *"Naked I came into this world and naked I'll leave. Blessed be the name of the Lord."*

The one question Job wanted an answer to is the same question many ask when they suffer loss. Why? Why I am going through this? Why did God let this happen? While suffering in the greatest way imaginable, his friends offered him no hope. In fact, the answer they gave was that it was his fault and he was hiding sin he had committed. If you get nothing else from this section, don't do this to someone who is suffering. Looking for who is to blame is rarely helpful when people are suffering. Sometimes, no one is to blame. I'm not sure why some feel comforted when blame is realized, but it is rarely the solution grieving people are searching for. Job grieved. He tore his clothes. He mourned, but he never lost his perspective. This is why faith and faithfulness are so important when dealing with tragedy before it comes. Job was never given an answer to the one question he needed answered. We may not always find the answer to this question either. We rarely suffer alone. Look for ways to help others who are suffering with you. I will say it again, when we suffer, we should serve. This may be difficult at times, but the most rewarding efforts in life are usually the toughest to perform.

If we are prepared for anything, we can prevent anxiety. As I am writing, I have friends suffering tragedy right now I can't fathom going through. When friends or relatives pass away, the afterlife is something people always talk about. Always. I've yet to attend a funeral where the person delivering the speech didn't mention heaven, but rarely do they mention hell. At the risk of sounding cold-hearted, I want to share my perspective on when people bring up uncertainty about the eternity of someone has passed. I don't worry about it. In fact, I don't even think about it. I can't do anything to change the eternal destiny of someone who has passed. I'm not a judge, but I know the Judge. He's smarter than I am, and I trust His wisdom when it comes to eternity for everyone. Have you prepared yourself for grief? Have you prepared yourself for eternity? If you have prepared yourself for eternity, preparing yourself for grief is much easier.

> *When people are grieving, avoid giving them doubt. Silence is a better option.*

I have attended more funerals than I care to mention. I've listened to preachers proudly announce the future of faithful servants of God and I've listened to preachers awkwardly try to convince family members their child a pronounced atheist at the time of a young death is in a better place. While most have been similar, a few stand out. I attended a funeral where no prayers were said. It was okay, I just wasn't accustomed to not hearing prayers. Perhaps the most interesting thing I've heard at a funeral was, "He is *probably* up in heaven right now." Probably? Really? I'm not sure how this was supposed to make the family feel, but it made me feel uncomfortable. When people are grieving, avoid giving them doubt. Silence is a better option.

I've mentioned I don't like funerals. In fact, I don't plan to have one when I die. I don't think it is wrong to have a funeral, but not for me. There are many reasons people choose to have a funeral. Some are cultural. Some are spiritual. Some are for family. Funerals are an expense at a time when people need to be focused on other things. This is my opinion. You are certainly free to disagree.

I want people to have a fun time when I pass and not worry or be anxious about what to wear to my funeral. I don't want them to have to travel any distance or spend a whole day agonizing over my absence, but rather celebrate a life well-lived. I enjoy every day I have breath and I don't live with anxiety. I want this anxiety-free approach to life to be what others remember and implement in their own lives.

If I'm not anxious about my own death, I don't want anyone else to be anxious either.

How does someone prepare themselves for tragedy or develop a mindset that allows them to grieve without living with anxiety? The T.R.I.A.L.S. method is a way to focus on others instead of on ourselves before and during tragic circumstances. As in every area of life, when we focus on others, we are the benefactors. It may sound strange to make goals for how we deal with tragedy, but preparing ourselves for everything requires us to set achievable goals.

Transparency: In the midst of tragedy, transparency is vital. Expressing our feelings can take a great deal of courage but is helpful to the body and soul. Releasing tension, hostility, anger, and any other emotions we experience during the grieving process will help our grief not become anxiety. If we create a lifestyle of transparency, it is easier to open up during tragedy. It will be difficult to be vulnerable if we feel forced to do this during trials. Remember, secrets create internal stress. Secrets don't cause others stress, they cause us stress.

If you are the support system for a suffering friend or family member, you must be approachable. You must be transparent, while at the same time remaining calm. Maintaining self-control is always a good thing.

Responsibility: During every trial, we have responsibilities. It may be work, family, finance, or responsibility within the trial itself. We are responsible to ourselves and may have responsibilities to others. Even when stress is at its peak, we must be aware of what they are. In addition, we must have the wherewithal to carry them out. If we are unsure of what we should do, ask someone. This is part of being responsible and transparent at the same time.

Intentionality: Being prepared for grief doesn't happen on accident. We must make a plan. We prepare for our finances, jobs, families, faith, etc. Planning for grief may sound like a dreary thing to do, but it is sensible. We can't gracefully breeze through difficulties in life without intentionally planning for how we respond to adversity. It is inevitable. We will experience pain and difficulty. If we are intentional about preparing ourselves for when it comes, we can limit our time of grief and avoid anxiety.

Appreciation: Living a life full of gratitude allows us to focus on others. I live every day making sure those closest to me to know how much I appreciate them. I am surrounded by people I love to serve, and I am thankful these same people serve each other. When we have opportunity to help others through the grieving process, we must be thankful for the opportunity to serve their needs. If we will look for ways to serve others when we are grieving, gratitude will be the result.

Limits: Knowing our limits helps us prepare for grief and potentially avoid circumstances that can turn into trials. When it comes to grief, we must communicate our limits to others who may be trying to help us. For example, if we need to grieve alone, we find a kind way to tell others we appreciate their willingness, but time alone is our preference in the moment. If our approach to grief is serving others, we also need to be aware of how much we can give when we are hurting. Over exertion can be just as harmful as the actual grief we are experiencing. Knowing our limits and communicating them to others is a great way to prepare ourselves before trials come.

Simplify: The process of simplifying life helps in every situation, especially when we deal with grief. After we realize our limits, we must find ways to reduce potential stressors in our life. When we need help, we must ask for help. If people offer help, allow them the blessing of caring for you. When you have a chance to help others simplify by caring for their needs when they grieve, serve. Just serve.

Motivation: Look at the different areas of the T.R.I.A.L.S. method and decide which of these is the hardest for you to implement in your life as you prepare yourself for potential grievous situations. Write down two ways you will put them into practice in your daily routine.

Advice: Serve others who suffer. Don't forget to grieve but serve when you suffer. This isn't always easy. It goes against nature, but it's helpful and it works. Develop a mindset to serve others regardless of life's circumstances and you will minimize your time of grief so it doesn't develop into anxiety.

Prayer: Lord, I understand trials are a part of life. Help me to always be prepared for expected and unexpected trials. When I suffer, help me to be vulnerable enough to lean on You and Your people. When others suffer, may I allow them to lean on me. I want to be outward focused, self-less, and helpful to others so that life without anxiety is possible for me and those I am surrounded by. Amen.

Chapter 10 – Prayer

Have you ever done something really stupid? Have you ever put yourself in a position where you knew the grace of God was the only means of escape for the poor decision you made? When I was in college, I went to Honduras on a mission trip. I was there to build houses, distribute food, and teach for seven days. After all the hard work, our group was rewarded with a three-day trip to Roatán, an island in Honduras with coral reef more beautiful than you can imagine, unless you've been there. In fact, we were told it was the second-best reef in the world.

I went with a group of Hondurans to snorkel and later learned the adventure involved swimming through some caves. We arrived at the first cave and I was last to swim through. I swam down about ten feet to the entrance of the cave, and the beauty I saw took my breath away. I was forced to swim back to the surface. A smart person would have realized how dangerous and foolish it was to swim though the cave, but not me. I took the deepest breath possible and swam back down. As I made my way through the cave, admiring the beauty of my surroundings, I failed to realize I was twice the size of the men who swam through before me, and I got stuck. Without exception, I have never been so scared in my life. I began moving rocks and sucking in my stomach as best I could. I squirmed and wiggled and did all I could to break free. In the midst of my struggle, I remember praying, "Lord, if you will get me out of this situation, I will never do something so stupid again." This sounds like a flippant prayer, but it is a promise I kept. God didn't miraculously save me but allowed me the ability and opportunity to free myself from the tight situation and I escaped.

> *"Lord, if you will get me out of this situation, I will never do something so stupid again."*

When you think about the worst or most irresponsible decision you made, how did you respond? Did you try to fix it on your own? Did you pray? Are you still dealing with consequences for those actions? Did your worst decision involve your spouse, kids, job, finances, health or faith? The foundation for overcoming anxiety in every area of life is prayer. This entire book is connected to a problem and a solution. Philippians 4:6 tells us to be anxious for nothing. This is a problem for many people because anxiety seems to be inevitable. The second half of this verse gives us a solution and result. Paul says, *"in everything with prayer and supplication, let your requests be made known to God and the peace that surpasses all understanding will guard your hearts and minds in Christ Jesus."*

> *If anxiety is the problem and prayer is the solution, we better know how to pray.*

Peace is the opposite of anxiety. How many sleepless nights have you experienced because of having peace in your life? Probably not many, if any. If anxiety is the problem and prayer is the solution, we better know how to pray. I want to emphasize that overcoming anxiety requires more than prayer. While prayer is important, it is just the foundation. The T.R.I.A.L.S. method accompanied with prayer is a catalyst for faith in action to prevent stress from becoming anxiety.

Philippians 4:6 mentions two of the five Greek words translated into our English word prayer: *proseuchumai* and *deesis*. Clearly, understanding prayer is a vital component of overcoming anxiety. We will discuss both of these areas as we strive to better understand what God expects of us when we communicate with Him.

What do you believe about the power of prayer? What is your reaction when circumstances change for the better? Do you pat yourself on the back and realize how great you are for your accomplishments? I have. Is it difficult to reject credit when something good happens? It feels good to achieve success. Good grades are expected after studying. It feels good to hear that you are great at something. What about when circumstances are not good? How do you respond when you don't get good grades after studying? How do you respond when you deserve a raise, but you get fired or someone else gets the raise and you are overlooked? Thinking about these situations can put us in a bad mood, and we look for someone to blame.

If the foundation for avoiding anxiety is prayer, it isn't enough just to know how to pray but to put it into practice. As we consider five areas of prayer, keep this question in the back of your mind: If you spent as much time talking to the most important person in your life as you do with God, what would the relationship look like? Many say the most important relationship in their life is God, but their actions may say something different. Let's break this down by the numbers. If you pray for twenty minutes each day, that is two hours and twenty minutes per week. How would your significant other feel if he or she got only two hours and twenty minutes of your time each week? How can you expect to have a great relationship with anyone based on this kind of time commitment? While men and women may answer the question differently, more communication never hurts.

I love prayer and teaching about prayer. It is always a time of self-reflection. I am forced to consider my own prayer life and how I need to improve. Can your prayer life use improvement? I have taught many classes on this subject and I ask groups, "How many of you pray too much?" I've yet to see a hand go up. There is no standard amount of time we should pray. We certainly shouldn't compare ourselves to one another because prayer is not a competition. Comparing our prayer life to that of another requires judgment of someone's heart. You are not a judge. Prayer is part of our daily goal to grow closer to God and eliminate anxiety in our life. I pray you will grow daily.

There are five areas of prayer we need to focus on as we develop our relationship with God: Adoration, confession, thanksgiving, supplication, and intercession. Within each of these areas, we see the need to be specific. It is helpful to compare our physical relationships to our relationship with God, so we have a more concrete point of view of the necessity to be specific when we approach our heavenly Father. I will compare my relationship with my wife to my prayer life. Pick your most important relationship while considering the questions in each section.

Adoration: This involves telling God what we think of Him. We have an example in Matthew 11:25 when Jesus spoke to God. Jesus says, "*I praise Thee, O Father . . .*" Psalm 145 is entirely about speaking to God with adoration. I remember attending church camp in Alaska when I was a child. An older teen led a prayer in our cabin, and he spoke to God as though he were speaking to a friend. The verbiage he used was cool in my mind. In addition to other terms, He told God He was awesome and cool. Without a doubt, God is both. At the same time, it seemed a little irreverent. Always consider who God is when expressing praise to His name.

As we express our adoration to anyone, especially God, we must be specific. My wife knows I think she is the most beautiful woman in the world. She is. She also knows I love her. She is kind, patient, thoughtful, considerate, an excellent cook, and an outstanding mother to our children. She models the woman mentioned in Proverbs 31. The list could go on and on. Just because she knows I believe all these things does not give me an out for communicating them less to her. If you are unsure if your wife wants to hear you praise her verbally, let me help you. She does! If you think your husband doesn't want to hear how strong, handsome, kind, thoughtful and charming he is, let me help you. He does! Be honest when giving praise. Don't say it unless you mean it. Positive communication is a good relationship builder and necessary for creating an environment that produces quality time together.

Can you guess where this section is going? When we speak to God, it is obvious He knows what we think of Him. He's omniscient. Just because He knows how we feel about Him, does not mean the need to tell Him is unnecessary. Expressing our feelings to God is for our benefit. More than anything, it shows a spirit of humility required to acknowledge His greatness above our own. Let us learn to use our words wisely and humbly as we express the greatness of our God. Be specific.

Confession: This involves telling our sins to God. My favorite text related to confession is in 1 John 1:7 – 9. It says, "*But if we walk in the light as He Himself is in the light, we have fellowship with one another and the blood of Jesus His Son cleanses us from all sin. If we say that we have no sin, we are deceiving ourselves and the truth is not in us. If we confess our sins, He is faithful and righteous to forgive us our sins and to cleanse us from all unrighteousness.*" This is great news. We can live without anxiety when we make mistakes if we will confess them to our God.

This is also true in our physical relationships. Let's imagine I am driving home from work and get pulled over for being the fastest car on the road. The grand prize? A 300-dollar ticket. While the kind officer is writing my ticket, one of my wife's friends sees what is going on and calls Kristen to make sure I am okay. I return home and she asks if I am okay and I respond everything is fine. She then asks, "Is there anything you want to tell me?" Gentlemen, always think before you answer this question; it can be loaded. If my response is, "Please forgive me for all the wrong things I've done," there is a zero percent chance she is going to be satisfied with that response.

In the first place, I haven't acknowledged my mistake. I haven't *yet* admitted I earned a speeding ticket and our tight budget just got a little tighter because I was trying to get home thirty seconds sooner. Secondly, I haven't asked for forgiveness. Whatever the wrong is, it must be admitted, repented of and then we must ask for forgiveness. Remember, keeping secrets causes anxiety for the person keeping them.

In our relationship with God, being specific with our confession is vital to having a great relationship. How many times do we pray or hear at the end of a prayer, "Please forgive us for all the wrong things we have done. In Jesus' name, Amen." These words are sometimes said with such velocity it's almost like a one-syllable sentence. Do we really feel contrite when we ask for forgiveness in this way? I doubt it. The opening prayer of an assembly dedicated to edification of God's people is not the time to confess our individual sins publicly. Preparing the assembly's mind for participating in the Lord's Supper is not the time to educate the group on all our shortcomings from the prior week, month, year, etc. However, if there is sin in our life, we must make time to talk to God about it and let Him know how penitent we are. This is not for God's benefit. He already knows of our sin. This is for our benefit and if we believe 1st John 1, it will feel as though the weight of the world is lifted off our shoulders when we ask God to forgive us for specific sin in our life.

Thanksgiving: This one is self-explanatory. It also happens to be a direct part of the T.R.I.A.L.S. lifestyle. Living a life centered on gratitude is one of the key elements in preventing anxiety. Expressing appreciation to God for what He has provided us involves humility in admitting we have needs. Do we need God? Do we rely on God? These sound like simple questions, but our answers are not often reflected in the way we live our lives. How often do we thank God for our jobs that allow us to earn an income to provide for ourselves and our families? Do we really believe God is responsible for our opportunities? How specific are we when we speak to God?

Let's get hypothetical one more time. My wife decides to send me and a friend on a golfing trip to Pebble Beach for a week to play golf and relax. I'm not sure where she got the money to do this, but this is hypothetical, so it doesn't matter. I have the time of my life. I'm stress free and living my best life. When I return, I give her a hug and say, "Thanks for all the things you have given me." Is this going to be sufficient gratitude? I don't know about your spouse, but this won't work for mine, nor should it. This woman took care of our four kids all under the age of ten, made an obvious financial sacrifice and allowed me to have a care-free week of relaxation. Taking care of the four kids alone involves more details that merit my gratitude than I can list. If the goal is a great relationship, I must be specific when I express gratitude.

Your relationship with God is the same. If the goal is a great relationship, you must be specific. Have you ever thanked God for indoor plumbing? For your toilet? For the specific car you drive, the closet full of clothes, diapers for your kids, wipes, the ability to provide so you don't have to do without the necessities of life? Have you heard the song, "Count your blessings, name them one by one"? Have you ever done that? If you wrote down every blessing you can think of, how many pieces of paper would you need? It would depend on how specific you are. Like confession, this is for our benefit, not the benefit of our creator and provider. James 1:17 says all good gifts come from our Heavenly Father. Let's be a people who are specific with our gratitude, knowing where our blessings come from.

Supplication: This is asking God for what we need. Supplication mandates we know the difference between our needs and wants. James 1 helps us understand the trials of life and our attitude toward them. He says in 1:5, *"But if any of you lacks wisdom, let him ask of God, who gives to all men generously and without reproach, and it will be given to Him."* Without question, everyone needs more wisdom, especially when it comes to dealing with anxiety. One of the many good gifts that come from our heavenly Father is the wisdom to deal with the trials we encounter in life.

Jesus taught His followers to pray for their daily bread, not enough food to supply for a few weeks. I'm not saying it is wrong to have a pantry full of food, but we need to recognize that as a want, rather than a need. In 1 Timothy 2, Paul encourages Timothy to pray for those in positions of authority. He doesn't specify that we pray for them only if we like and agree with them; he says to pray for them. This is for our own good. We need people in authority.

God is a mind reader. He knows your mind and He knows your heart. I am not a mind reader, and neither is my bride. When it comes to my needs, I must communicate them clearly to her. Remember the "T" in T.R.I.A.L.S.? Transparency is essential when expressing our needs in our physical relationships. It is also essential when asking God to meet our needs. While God already knows what we need, telling our specific needs to God creates a bond of honesty and recognition that we depend on our Creator. When you pray, make a list of your needs. Before making this list, read Mathew 6:25 – 34. You will find your list of needs is much shorter than your wants. When you have a grasp on the difference between your needs and your wants, you become aware of how truly blessed you are by God.

Intercession: This is asking God for the needs of others. In Ephesians 6, we are taught to pray or make petitions for all the saints. James 5 teaches we are to confess our sins one to another and to pray for each other. Why? The text says the result is healing. What a blessing to know God gives us the opportunity to help heal other people through our prayers. Praying was never intended to be a selfish act. In John 17, Jesus prayed for his followers to be unified. This includes you and me.

Many examples throughout the New Testament show the apostles praying for each other and the church. In Philippians 1, Paul mentions he thanked God upon every remembrance of the saints in Philippi. Do you think Paul really prayed that much for these people? I do. You should pray for your brothers and sisters and their needs. You should be specific. These prayers must also be joined by the action of telling your brothers and sisters you are praying for them. This communication will build relationships and create a bond of unity only found in Christ. May we all be a people who are concerned for each other and bring our concern before God to help us in our time of need.

What does God expect when we pray?

In Isaiah 66:2, God states, *"But to this one I will look. To him who is humble and contrite of spirit, and who trembles at My Word."* God expects us to recognize who He is and who we are when we speak to Him. Far too often, we bring God down to our level or we elevate ourselves to His level when we are speaking to Him. Humility is a requirement to approach the Creator of the universe. We do not deserve for Him to listen to us, but He does. In Luke 18, Jesus addresses a group of Pharisees who thought they were better than everyone else. He tells a story of two men who pray at the temple. One of them was an arrogant man who prided himself on his obedience. Can you imagine being arrogant about obeying God? The other man wasn't willing to lift his head but asked God to be merciful because he was unworthy. God rewarded the man who was humble and contrite. Pride and arrogance will always be a detriment in our communication to God.

Misconceptions in Prayer:

We began this chapter looking at what we believe about the power of prayer. Sadly, many who use it only as a last resort. Have we ever said, "All I can do is pray"? I have. Is that the way we value prayer? Do we attempt to use every resource we have to fix every problem on our own and when we fail, we turn to God? This is not the way prayer was designed.

At the end of a football game, when the score is close and the team with the ball needs a last second touchdown in order to tie or win the game, the quarterback heaves the ball as hard as he can into the end zone and hopes one of his players makes a miraculous catch. It is called a "Hail-Mary" pass. It is a last-ditch effort because the team wasn't successful in their attempts for the previous fifty-nine minutes and fifty-five seconds. This is not the way prayer was designed.

When I was a kid, Shaquille O'Neal was drafted to play in the NBA. He became famous as one of the biggest players to play the game. He also became famous for the name or phrase "hack a Shaq." He was unstoppable in the post area, but he had one of the worst free-throw percentages of everyone in the entire league. I can't imagine getting paid millions and millions of dollars and not being able to make a free-throw but that's another story. When he went to the free-throw line, I often thought, "He doesn't have a prayer". What does that mean? He doesn't have hope. Is that how we feel about prayer? Do we hope God hears us? Do we hope He answers us? When we approach the throne of God almighty, we need to have confidence. Hebrews 4:16 says we should have confidence when we approach God. There is a great difference between arrogance and confidence.

We must believe God hears and answers our prayers. This is one of the purposes of the entire book of Hebrews. Jesus is better than Moses because He gives us a direct line to God the Father. If we approach on our own, our arrogance will hinder our prayers. If we approach through Jesus, we should have confidence God hears us.

The last misconception I want to mention about prayer is, "A family that prays together, stays together." Prayer is not a bonding agent. It will not magically force people to get along and never disagree. Plenty of families prayed together and tragedy or poor decision-making caused division. Prayer must be a fundamental part of every family, but it alone will not hold a family together. Application of the T.R.I.A.L.S. method and prayer together offer a solution to help when anxiety becomes evident in the lives of individuals or families.

Effective Communication

Effective communication requires a clear relationship. We must remove barriers, so that we can have an open line with those to whom we are speaking. In prayer, this means we don't multi-task. If the only time we spend in prayer is when we are driving down the road, I hope we believe God hears us when our eyes are open. It is great to have our mind constantly focused on God, even when we are driving. However, we must make quiet, personal time, free from distraction if we want to have a clear line of communication. How well would our spouse react if the only time we communicated was while we had our eyes glued to a phone, TV, or computer? How effective would that make our communication? Don't multi-task when praying.

Effective communication also requires time. Bits and pieces of your busy life will not suffice if your desire is a great relationship with God. If you make the time to carefully go through the five areas of prayer discussed in this chapter, it requires more than three minutes each day. Make a habit of writing out your prayers or make a list of what you want to talk to God about. If you feel you can't make twenty or thirty minutes each day, start with five minutes. Make a prayer schedule if going through all five areas is too much in one day. For example, make Monday prayers all about the church since they may be fresh on your mind. Pray for the leadership. Pray for the ministries and outreach. Pray for ambition to be involved in ministry areas when you are not involved. Make Tuesday about gratitude and write down fifty things for which you are thankful. If that's too many, come up with twenty and thank God for each one specifically. On Wednesday, talk to God about what you need. Be specific. Make your way through the week and focus on a different area each day if that helps keep your attention where it needs to be. Make a plan and get to work on your prayer life. It is essential to overcoming anxiety.

Conditions of Prayer

Four conditions of prayer must be realized before we approach the throne of God. The first deals with motives.

James 4:3 – 6 says, *"You ask and do not receive, because you ask with wrong motives, so that you may spend it on your pleasures. You adulteresses, do you not know that friendship with the world is hostility toward God? Therefore, whoever wishes to be a friend of the world makes himself an enemy of God. Or do you think that the scripture speaks to no purpose: He jealously desires the Spirit which He has made to dwell in us? But He gives a greater grace. Therefore, it says, God is opposed to the proud but gives grace to the humble."*

Our approach must be humility and selflessness when talking to God. If our expectation is receiving the unmerited favor of our Creator, it allows us to understand the need of God's will to be done, not ours.

The second component is praying for God's will to be done. Can we pray for things that go against God's will? I suppose we can pray for them, but we shouldn't expect God to grant us things that violate His will. If I pray for the ability to fly, should I be shocked when I can't fly? God put the law of gravity into effect for our safety. He isn't going to change that because I want to fly. Flying would be awesome, but it isn't going to happen. Pray for something else. If we are unsure about the will of God in relationship to our requests, pray for wisdom to accept the answer we receive. We should do this whether we are sure or not.

We must also ask in faith. James 1:5 instructs us to ask for wisdom. Continue reading and you find that the next verse says to ask in faith if we wish to receive. Doubt is one of Satan's tools that makes us unstable and unable. If we ask without faith, why waste the breath? Jesus says in Matthew 21:22 – 22, *"Truly I say to you, if you have faith and do not doubt, you shall not only do what was done to the fig tree but even if you say to this mountain, 'Be taken up and cast into the sea, it shall happen.' And all things you ask in prayer, believing, you shall receive."* Faith is a vital component to our prayer life.

Without Jesus, prayer is not possible. In John 14:6, Jesus says, *"I am the way, the Truth and the Life and no one comes to the Father except through me."* Praying in Jesus' name is the final condition of prayer. This does not mean you have to end your prayer with the words "in Jesus's name, Amen." In fact, prayer in scripture ends this way. Throughout the New Testament, we see the phrase "calling on the name of the Lord." "Name" is the same Greek word as our English word, authority. It is because of the authority of Jesus we can pray. Jesus gives us this right as His people.

After obtaining the knowledge of the components, misconceptions, and conditions of prayer, you must decide to put wisdom to action. Pray more. If you are uncertain what words to say when you approach God, read prayers from the Bible. Ask leaders in your church for help. I've mentioned my email address in a few chapters but here it is again: turnerc23@yahoo.com . Send me a message if you need some help getting started with your new prayer life. Your words are important, but your spirit and heart are more important.

The T.R.I.A.L.S. method is a great complement to a consistent prayer life and will aid you in overcoming anxiety. In your prayers, consider how each area will be utilized as you grow in your faith, and relationship to God.

Transparency: God already knows everything about you. Open your heart, be honest with yourself as you confess sin, gratitude, and needs to your heavenly Father. He who hears in secret will reward you. Keep in mind, specificity within the context of confession and gratitude is for our benefit, not God's. Watch your relationship grow.

Responsibility: Your prayer life is your responsibility. Families should pray together. Spouses should pray together, but everyone should have a personal relationship with their Creator. Can you imagine relying on someone else to communicate to God for you? God can't either. Be an example to your friends and family of a person after God's own heart. Pray often.

Intentionality: A great prayer life doesn't happen by accident. You must be intentional with your time. Create time in your day for God. Every word we utter to God must be intentional. Mindless repetition is rebuked in scripture. Why would it be acceptable today? Talking to God is not to be fitted into our life. Our life must be centered on prayer. Find peace that comes through prayer and you will eliminate anxiety.

Appreciation: Having a thankful heart is one of the key components to a successful prayer life. Show God gratitude in your words but also in your daily life by how you treat others. Be a servant. Thank God in the way He wants to be thanked, not the way it is easiest for you show thanks. Learn God's love language and express it all the time. Develop an attitude of gratitude.

Limits: Knowing your limits is all about time and timing. If your limits are pushed and you run out of time to talk to God, it is time to slow down. If you have trouble with limits, make a check list. Put prayer at the top, in the middle and at the bottom of your checklist. Put reminders around your house and place of work to help avoid pushing physical limits so that your spiritual limits don't get pushed either.

Simplify: When you reduce physical distractions, you will find more time for prayer. When limits are bursting at the seams, we must stop, breathe, and find a way to get rid of the noise. Find help. A simple life is a life of tranquility and peace. We don't have to be on the go all the time. If we don't have time to pray, we have big problems. Add simplicity, reduce anxiety.

Motivation: Make a prayer list. Write down all the areas discussed in this chapter (adoration, confession, thanksgiving, supplication and intercession). Add seven items under each area and talk to God about the items on your list. Do this every day for a week.

Advice: Pray every night. Try to fall asleep praying. If you don't utter or even think the words "in Jesus name, amen," don't worry, He still hears your prayer. Pray every morning. When your vision is blurry, when your stomach is growling, pray. Be thankful for each day.

Prayer: Father, You are awesome, holy, mighty, faithful and creator of every good thing. Thank you for prayer. Thank you for allowing your unworthy servant to talk to you and for the confidence I have in knowing you hear and answer my concerns. Help me grow in my faith and my faithfulness to you. Be with my family and my friends. Help me to be grateful and content with the abundance you have given me. May your Spirit move through me every moment of every day, and may Your will be done in my life. Amen.

Chapter 11 – Leadership and Anxiety

Have you ever wondered how the most accomplished leaders deal with stress and anxiety? Do they have any? Some lead fearlessly and seem to run such a tight ship no space is left for anxiety. Nearly every picture of leaders in action promotes an upbeat person with a smile, demanding an audience give their undivided attention, as they deliver a life-changing message. This message has every attendee sitting on the edge of the seat. Is this you? Are you on the stage or in the crowd? Where do you stand in leadership? Are you the leader or are you following someone? Does your role give you peace or anxiety?

> *". . . if unchecked worry usually leads us to the very place we didn't want to go – it leads to a semblance of failure"*
> *– John Maxwell*

"Anxiety is one of the top nemeses to a leader (and all humans for that matter). This issue can paralyze the progress of any organization. After years of working with CEO's and business owners I have noticed that we all have a pattern for dealing with worry and that pattern needs to be broken. Here is how it usually works... First, worry sets in around pressure (usually financial or unmet expectations). Second, it begins to fester and take on more influence than it deserves in our minds. Third, we begin to change the way we behave. For most men I have noticed that we internalize it and clam up. We become more quiet in general and short in our conversations. Fourth, worry begins to affect the way we think. Pressure mounts and we begin to be very short term in our strategy and thinking. Finally, if unchecked worry usually leads us to the very place we didn't want to go - it leads to a semblance of failure" (John Maxwell).

My story

Everyone fails at some point in life. The lesson learned drives or debilitates the one who fails. I have had the fortunate pleasure of starting at the bottom of a company and working my way to the top. When I was fifteen, I worked in the warehouse of swimming pool company. As far as corporate ladders go, I was at the bottom. No one worked for less money than I did. Sounds encouraging, right? Over the course of five years, I worked my way up to one of most important people at our branch. I hired people. I had to fire one employee for sleeping upstairs in a hot warehouse while on the clock. He was found by one of the owners of the business who was in town analyzing our branch. Shortly thereafter, the company decided to close the doors and the current manager opened his own pool store. After graduating college, I went back to work with my former boss as the manager of his new store. I spent years learning every aspect of this business from warehouse organization, inventory, installing, sales, water chemistry to store re-location. The part of work I loved the most was customer service, and it was my most challenging task. We had 600 customers and I knew most of them by name. Keeping them happy all the time was a chore. Talk about stress!

While working my way up the ladder in this business, I would have said I was a good leader. The more experience and knowledge I gained, the more I thought I was worth. Insecurity began to creep in, and leadership qualities were not present. In fact, I began to do everything I could to make myself irreplaceable. I thought if I could do everything, my boss wouldn't want to get rid of me. I was not going to teach someone else all I knew because then I wouldn't be as valuable. I wasn't there to grow the business, I was there to keep my job and make as much money as I could. If the company grew as a result, that was a bonus. In hindsight, I was a terrible leader. I was self-serving and there only for the paycheck. This is not the way to be successful or a good leader. The truth is everyone can be replaced.

Shortly after my ninth year in this industry, I was offered a job in a non-profit ministry. Because I wasn't looking for a career change, the call caught me a little off guard. Job titles were never important to me, but because only one other person was working in this ministry, I was starting high up the ladder. Reading the list of job responsibilities was exhausting. Most of the responsibilities required a computer and knowledge of how to use one. This presented a real problem. At twenty-five years of age, I had never owned a computer. Oh, how times have changed!

After nine years in a non-profit ministry, which has grown at astronomical rates, I have learned a tremendous amount about leadership on both ends of the spectrum. Growth on every level requires change. Leaders change, followers change, and organizations change. Our ministry has experienced change more in the last nine years than I ever imagined it would or could. There were growing pains as I adjusted to working under the oversight of a group of elders. I was accustomed to being number two in command in my previous job, for no one else was directly involved in our ministry.

In my working career, I have had the opportunity to be in unique positions of leadership, and stress has been evident every step of the way. I had the stress of managing a large customer database. I was yelled at, cussed at, and watched people ache while spending countless dollars on a luxury most only dream to enjoy. Our non-profit ministry, Spanish Missions, started with about three thousand students in 2008 and now has over thirty thousand. In 2008, there were 2.8 million downloads, and in 2017, there were over 30 million. We have grown.

Every year, we sit down and make a list of goals and expectations for our ministry. We do this in our family and recommend you do this as well. Goal setting is a key component of growth, but it isn't enough. We must make a plan to reach our goals. I love revisiting old lists of goals and seeing how much tangible growth we have experienced as a ministry and as individuals.

I've mentioned our ministry operates under the oversight of elders. While I have always known them to be men of wisdom and experience, I haven't always agreed with their decisions. That doesn't mean they were wrong; it means we disagreed. Disagreements are often accompanied by stress and anxiety. Two years into my ministry career, I thought it necessary to move to Colorado for eight weeks to study at a preaching school. I had a plan. I would study during the day and work at night. This ministry allows me to work in remote locations when needed. Because my parents lived close to the school, I wouldn't have to pay for a place to stay. All that was left to do was to ask the elders what they thought.

Have you ever intentionally stepped on a bug and squashed it like the miserable, bothersome creation it was? After asking the elders what they thought of my plans, I felt like the bug and viewed them as the boot that did the squashing. A little stress was involved in asking because of the unknown response. The clarity of their response brought anxiety and frustration. How do you deal with people you view as making irrational decisions that don't support plans you made? As a leader, how do you deal with those following you who make irrational requests? It's tough. I was a grown man, at least in my own estimation. I had no clue they wouldn't celebrate with me the possibility of growing in my knowledge and leaving town for two months. It was heart-breaking.

It didn't take long before I realized the wisdom in their decision. I never had intentions of moving to Denver and quitting the ministry but perhaps that was one of their fears. Fear causes anxiety and skepticism. They spent the last several years looking for the right person to do this job, not to mention the amount of money they had invested in potential candidates that didn't work out. I can only imagine their skepticism of me the first few years we worked together. I never gave them any reason to doubt my commitment, but I now understand the importance of those first several years. A day will come when I look for someone to help me in this ministry and I'm already preparing myself for the process.

Not only have I been at the bottom of leadership and in the middle, working under the oversight of some great men, I currently serve as the Spanish minister for a local congregation. While I appreciate all the help offered within this ministry, I am the only bilingual person in a leadership position. I get asked every question. I get called every time someone needs a visit. I do all the teaching. God has been more than gracious to provide a couple who desire to help. Thankfully, one of them leads singing every Sunday. If I led singing every week, our numbers would likely decrease. How do you minister daily in the lives of twenty to thirty people while working full-time in a ministry with over thirty thousand students, under the oversight of another group of men, and maintain balance within the home as a leader and provider? T.R.I.A.L.S.

Stress and Anxiety

Every organization, corporation, business, and ministry has a leadership component. Most have layers of leadership which make nearly everyone responsible for working with or for someone. Whether there are two or two hundred employees, stress is inevitable. We all put pressure on ourselves and others to make sure tasks are done appropriately and efficiently. Opinions, personalities, and experiences all vary, making it seem impossible to complete some of the smallest projects. Deadlines are not met, stress escalates, most of the team is now dealing with anxiety, and the boss is lurking around the corner with steam coming from his ears because the company does not function at an optimal level. Sound familiar?

Stress is not always avoidable. When more than one person is involved, stress is present regardless of the task. It may be unspoken, but it is there. However, anxiety is still optional. How you respond to stress determines how much peace you enjoy. Often, it determines how you sleep at night. Maintaining a helpful and positive perspective during stressful circumstances is not always easy, but it is rewarding. Like all the areas of life we looked at, we must consider the thoughts and opinions of others as we strive to avoid anxiety within leadership.

In every aspect of leadership, help is needed. Reliance is needed. This requires humility and service. Asking for help is one of the most difficult aspects of leadership, but one of the most necessary. When we ask others for help, we must be willing to serve them. Having the heart to serve in all circumstances is so important. If some people are unwilling to serve within our context, leadership is going to be difficult. Our service elevates the performance of others. Serve.

Jesus was the Son of God in the flesh, and He asked for the help of twelve men to send a message to the entire world. He performed miracles the world had never seen and will never see again. He was the greatest leader the world has ever seen and continues to influence more lives than any person in history. In John 13, we read about Jesus washing the feet of these men and giving them advice on how to lead. We must communicate, love, serve and love. If one of those sounds repetitious, read John 13. Jesus says it over and over. Love people, especially each other.

Even with the best service in every capacity, stress can still be present. The T.R.I.A.L.S. method is a lifestyle that reduces stress and eliminates anxiety in every situation. Untreated stress will turn into anxiety. Leadership is a lot like marriage. The three keys to successful leadership are communication, communication, and communication. The first step is transparency. The best leaders are always excellent communicators. Always.

Service-oriented leadership is the best way to influence others, but the choice to change is still theirs.

Before we discuss the process of eliminating anxiety in leadership, it is vital for every leader to know his/her purpose. Why are you a leader? What is your goal in all you do? When a leader understands why he/she is in this position, the next step is communicating to others. Every confrontation, disagreement, lack of performance, personality conflict and problem that arises must be handled by looking how it relates to the vision or the "why" of the organization. This is true in the home, world, and church. Regardless of your position, you are leading someone. It may be a spouse, children, employee, church member, or even a total stranger who happens to watch your example. You have influence.

Understanding influence is a key component to leadership. We cannot change people. We may do our best to make people do what we want, but we cannot change them. Our example and our words are tools that influence others. Service-oriented leadership is the best way to influence others, but the choice to change is still theirs. When we disagree with others, finding ways to incorporate more than one opinion will go a long way to resolve stress and avoid anxiety.

In his book, _Start with Why_, Simon Sinek addresses a main component of success. The book illustrates how Apple has been so successful in their industry. They have convinced people they don't want Apple products, but they need them. They cannot survive without them. When the vision is clear, when communication is transparent, when purpose is evident, when ambition is selfless, success is the result. Know your why and make sure those you work for, with, and over know the "why". Use these principles to guide you as a leader, and anxiety will work itself out of your life. It may not happen tomorrow, but it will happen.

Transparency: Good leaders teach others the need for transparency. Great leaders follow their own advice. If we live a life of transparency, why would we be anxious if others speak poorly of us? Can they bring a charge against us we are unaware of or that catches us off guard? Within the world, home and church, leaders must be transparent, and they must follow through. The best intentions don't mean much when the result is not what was promised. Transparency supersedes mistakes when we are honest. No one is perfect.

When you find yourself in a difficult or stressful situation, pause, and ask yourself if there is any information you can share with others to find peace. Remaining calm as we communicate will not escalate our stress levels. When others are getting heated and emotional, a calm spirit can diffuse a ticking bomb. Tranquility coupled with transparency is a combination for success when stress is getting close to anxiety.

Responsibility: When I hear the word "leadership," I think of responsibility. We make many decisions that bring us to our current reality. Some great decisions have helped promote our career. Bad decisions may exist that leave us with consequences to deal with for a long time. Regardless, we are responsible for how we got where we are at this time and place. We must understand our future is determined by how responsible we are in the moment. A healthy evaluation before each major decision within our leadership role is necessary if we want to avoid anxiety.

Have you made decisions you aren't proud of, but they helped you in your career? Are they decisions others know about? Do they need to know about them? Some mistakes are on a need to know basis and that's okay. However, the responsible action is one that helps us avoid drama and anxiety in the future. If faults need to be admitted, take care of them as soon as possible. Some responsible decisions may cost you a job or position in leadership. Transparency and responsibility will lay the foundation for believing vulnerability is better than anxiety. Both are choices we have the power to make.

Intentionality: As a leader, every decision counts. We will not escape anxiety by accident. We choose to avoid it. When others know our actions are intentional, it creates an atmosphere of preparation for each occasion. When confronted with the choice of whom to serve, Joshua says, *"As for me and my house, we will serve the Lord"* (Joshua 24:15). Every action and reaction are choices we make. Proper preparation leads to making the best choices.

Do you lead with intentionality? Do you find yourself in a leadership role but have doubts about your direction? Stop. Think. Read a book. Read this book. Consult those you trust as leaders who have been in your shoes. Analyze people, circumstances, and potential. When the right choice is evident, execute. Be confident and intentional.

Appreciation: The role of gratitude cannot be overstated for leaders. No one gets to the top without help. Learn to show gratitude to the least of those who have helped you and especially to the most important. We must develop an attitude of gratitude in every level of leadership. Whether we are thanking those above us or those who follow us, expressing appreciation is a relationship builder. Throughout scripture, we read the command to give thanks in all things. Above all, we are to thank God for the opportunity to serve as leaders in whatever community we find ourselves. Leadership is a responsibility and an honor. Be thankful.

Do you know great leaders who aren't thankful? I don't. If you want to be a great leader, this is a quality you must possess. If you are not accustomed to saying "thank you," start now. The most important aspect of gratitude is understanding how to show gratitude to those who merit our thanks. If you read the other chapters in this book, you are familiar with _The Five Love Languages_ by Gary Chapman. We should know those around us well enough to be familiar with how they want to be thanked. I worked in a business for several years and my boss thought giving me a paycheck was gratitude enough. After eight years of knowing him and helping create a successful company, I received a gift card to Golfsmith one year for my Christmas bonus. I don't want to sound ungrateful, but I would have rather had a hand written, heart-felt thank you card. Know your people. Express gratitude.

Limits: Have you ever wondered why we have speed limits? They are not for the road's sake but for our sake. Knowing speed limits is for our benefit. In leadership, we must know our limits in so many areas. The main area we must know our limits is time. We can cram only so much into our schedule. While airlines consider being overbooked a positive situation, it is not for leaders. People get upset, and we don't have a voucher to hand out when we under-deliver or fail to deliver on the promises of our time. Time management is vital to avoiding anxiety in leadership.

Have you ever wished you had more time? Would having more time really help you eliminate anxiety or would you pile more into your schedule because of the overflow? You must evaluate your priorities and be firm. If you have a primary job that pays your bills, this must be your priority, unless you don't need the job. Volunteer work is great, but not if it keeps you from commitments you make to your job or family. Serving your community is great. Serving your family is better. As a leader, you must evaluate you. You must evaluate your time and schedule.

Knowing our limits allows us to decline opportunities, even if we would rather accept. Professionally, I love public speaking. I love teaching and preaching as much as any other aspect of my ministry work. I get asked to speak on a variety of topics in places all over the U.S. and South and Central America. There are times when I get asked by two groups to speak on the same day. Which do I decline? There are other times when family time will be interrupted if I accept an invite to speak. I try to decline as many of these as possible. Know your priorities. Let your priorities know they are priorities.

Simplify: There is a reason simplifying is the final step in this process of eliminating anxiety. Before the volcano erupts, we must act. When turmoil begins to show up because we are out of time and have too many tasks to complete, we must stop and decide how we can excuse ourselves from some of these activities. This doesn't have to offend or upset others. In fact, it should do just the opposite. The hardest aspect of simplifying is the help it requires.

For years, I thought I had no limits. I could do it all. The older I get, the more I realize how foolish I was for thinking such. As much as I love to teach and preach, I live around the threshold of my limits. If someone were to ask me right now if I could teach a Bible study during the week, I must decline. Every time I say "yes" to one opportunity, I am saying "no" to another. Usually, because my family takes the hit on these occasions, I have decided not to push my limits. Simplifying is much easier. When I decline opportunities, I do my best to help find a replacement I trust.

Simplifying is also much easier when you are part of a well-connected team. Do you work with people you trust? Do you work with people you can count on to help when you are absent? It is vital to surround yourself with others who know the vision of your organization and are hands on and willing to participate whenever needed.

Motivation: Write down the most difficult situation you have been involved with in the past or currently. Walk through each area of the T.R.I.A.L.S. method and find the step that is missing or needs correcting to see how anxiety can be eliminated.

Advice: Get help. The greatest leaders all need help. Think of one person who is capable but has lacked opportunity. You know who the person is before you finish reading this. Give them a chance. Allow them to take some of the stress off your plate and watch teamwork eliminate potential anxiety.

Prayer: Lord, thank you for allowing me to be a leader. Help me to always realize a follower of Jesus is a leader. I have many responsibilities. Help me to realize the most important is leading others to You. When stress arises, help me to be transparent with myself and with others. You see all. I have no secrets from you. Forgive me when pride keeps me from asking for help and give me the strength and humility to incorporate others into my life when I need help. Amen.

Chapter 12 – Bringing it All Together

When I was a kid, I remember old people loved to talk about the weather. I always laughed when I heard them because I had no concern about the weather. A few years later, when I was in my twenties, we built our first house. There wasn't an hour that went by that I wasn't checking the weather. I was worried about lining people up and what would happen if I got behind. If there was even a chance of rain in the forecast, it was a real mental hurdle to get over. After building six houses, I realized it was all unnecessary because I can't control the weather. I must be willing to accept the results and consequences of elements of my life I can't control. If I take a deep breath and look at the big picture, it's going to work out. However, there were lots of things I could control. For example, if my plumber needed to show up in two weeks, I should probably call him and tell him I'll be ready in two weeks. If I wait until the day I need him and then call to let him know I'm ready, it isn't going to work out very well. It was in my control to call him ahead of time and be prepared. If I fail to prepare properly, I must be willing to accept the consequences for my own actions. Without a doubt, we end up with unnecessary pressure on ourselves if we do not plan ahead. This is what I mean when I say we, at times, choose to put stress and anxiety in our lives.

> *The key to overcoming anxiety is being prepared . . . for everything.*

The key to overcoming anxiety is being prepared...for everything. This may sound like an impossible task, but can you imagine waking up every morning not worried at all about anything that could come your way? The good news is it is a possibility. In fact, I do this every day. All we have to do is choose not to allow our mind, our attitude, and our happiness to be determined by factors outside our control. Sounds easy enough, right?

In the introduction to this book, I mentioned the importance of my faith. In fact, it is the most important thing in my life. Several years ago, I was asked to teach a course in Guatemala about a man named Job who lived long ago. He was the wealthiest person of his time in every regard. The Bible speaks well of him. He had a wife and ten children. He had more material possessions than everyone. In one single day, he lost everything but his wife. He became so ill he had to scrape the boils off his skin because of the intense pain. Life went from perfect to complete misery.

This was a religious man with his wife but they had different perspectives. If you look at them and their individual lives, the question they would answer differently is this: If you were to lose everything, would your faith be enough to keep you faithful? For Job, the answer was obvious. He never wavered in his faithfulness. His response to losing everything was, "the Lord gives and the Lord takes away. Blessed be the name of the Lord." His wife's response was, "Curse God and die." How would we respond?

Take a moment and let's evaluate stress. Before we place anything else in our life, we must consider if the potential anxiety of losing any given item is more costly than the current value of not having it. For example, if I want to buy an $80,000 car and I can afford it, great! If losing that car will create anxiety I cannot overcome, is it worth having the car? If I spend every minute of every day thinking about this car and how upset I will be if someone scratches or dents the car, is it worth having? I'm not suggesting we shouldn't be careful or that we shouldn't care about our possessions. I am suggesting we should have a healthy understanding of our own emotions and attitudes toward our possessions so that losing something that is temporary won't create stumbling blocks in our life.

> *Being normal is a stumbling block or common trial for all of us.*

**As mentioned in the chapter on life, being normal is a stumbling block or common trial for all of us. The standard by which we judge normal is often what we see on social media. If you don't use social media, I applaud you. If you use social media, I want to warn and enlighten you on some research that is telling of the direction of future generations. The purpose is never to condemn, but to instruct and prepare others for the future and the dangers of social media and the impact it has on anxiety.

According to research by Dr. Tim Elmore, every generation welcomes new technology. From baby boomers and their vinyl records to generation Z with their smart phones and apps for everything, the latest, greatest technology is on everyone's wish list. With each new generation, technology has become more pervasive, more private and more powerful (www.growingleaders.com). Keep in mind, secrets and privacy are major causes of anxiety. Research shows the growing influence and desire young people have to keep a screen in front of their face. Research suggests that people use a portable device an average of eighty times per day.

It is both sad and amazing how a few words posted on a social media status can change the way we feel about others and ourselves. We allow the thoughts and words of others to influence the way we feel about ourselves, our activities and the way we dress. The way we feel about our financial circumstances and our family members is also influenced by social media.

Timothy Turner's book, *Preaching to a Programmed People*, states the average American views over 29 hours of television each week (Turner, 1995). This much exposure to media of any sort changes the way we listen and view things off the screen such as sermons, lectures, leadership figures, etc. Most shows are thirty minutes long. The average attention span was twenty-three minutes but is even shorter now. Can you imagine why it is difficult to sit through a thirty-minute sermon by someone who lectures while standing in the same place?

Business solutions firm, LivePerson, just released the results of a poll after talking to 4,000 young people between eighteen and thirty-four years of age around the world to find out how much of their lives are lived out digitally. The vast majority of Millennials and Generation Z said they'd rather talk to someone online than in person. In the U.S., nearly 74% of respondents would rather send a text message instead of having a conversation in person. The majority of them (62%) would rather leave their wallet at home than their phone when going out. And a full 70% sleep with their phone next to them (liveperson.com).

How do you feel right now? Are you connected? I have asked large groups of people what they would do if they left their home to go an hour down the road and twenty minutes into their drive they realized they left their phone at home. Nearly every person said they would turn around and go home. What about you? Would you relax in the short disconnection from the technology driven world we live in or would you turn around to go re-attach yourself to a device you can't seem to live without for an hour?

The Pew Research Center claims that, "seven of ten Americans use social media to connect with one another, engage with news content, share information, and entertain themselves." When they began tracking social media adoption in 2005, just five percent of American adults used at least one of these platforms. By 2011, that share had risen to half of all Americans, and today 69% of the public uses some type of social media" (pewinternet.org).

These statistics should alarm all of us or at least cause us to be aware of where and how people engage in communication. While there are many positives to social media such as communicating from a distance, promoting business, enjoying a laugh; there is also a plethora of negatives. Perhaps the greatest negatives are bullying and the promotion of pornography.

In a survey by the Barna Research Group, questions were asked to five age groups in regard to how frequently they came across porn versus how often they seek out porn. The results are staggering:

1) Teens 12-17: 8% seek it out daily, 18% weekly, and 11% once or twice a month. Total of 37% of teens.
2) Young adults 18-24: 12% seek it out daily, 26% weekly, and 19% once or twice a month. A total of 57% actively seek out pornography.
3) Older millennials 25-30: 8% daily, 17% weekly, 18% once or twice a month. That is 42% total.
4) Gen-Xers 31-50: 7% daily, 16% weekly, 18% once or twice a month. Total is 41%.
5) Boomers 51-69: 2% daily, 7% weekly, 14% once or twice a month. Total is 23% (barna.com).

The greater problem is half of adults twenty-five years old and older don't believe it is wrong to view pornography. 45% believe it is wrong to read about it and only 37% believe it is morally wrong to watch sexually explicit material on television. The numbers are even worse among those between eighteen and twenty-four years of age. Between seven and eight out of every ten in this age group don't believe anything is wrong with viewing pornography. Leaders, it is time to stand up and put greater influences in the lives of our young people. We cannot be silent about this issue. We cannot accept this as the cultural "norm." Rid your vocabulary of the world's view of normal and be proactive in creating positive alternatives for your audience.

Bullying is also a growing trend of negativity in the lives of people who use social media. According to a January 2017 survey, 41% of Americans said they had experienced some form of online harassment. Among the ages of eighteen to twenty-nine, the share was 67% (pewinternet.org). To put this in perspective, if you and four of your friends are holding hands, statistically speaking, at least one of the hands you are holding has been harassed on social media.

The growing trend of arguing on social media has led to many cases of harassment. There are many reasons why people admit to engaging in this kind of behavior.

a) 26% say a stranger did not like what I posted.
b) 22% say someone I know did not like what I posted.
c) 19% say I was defending someone else in an argument.
d) 17% say I did not like what someone I know posted.
e) 17% say I did not like what a stranger posted (pewinternet.org).

I understand everyone wants to be heard and social media is a large platform, perhaps the largest in the world. Exercise caution when you post on social media. If you find yourself posting negative and hateful comments online, you need to do some self-reflection. Before posting your political, social, spiritual, physical or other point of view, ask yourself the question, "Has my mind ever been changed by reading someone's opinion on social media?" Mine hasn't either. Think before you post. Post positivity. Delete inappropriate comments. Do a social media fast and see how liberating it is not to worry about the thoughts and negativity that are posted far too often.

I'm a huge proponent of social media when it is used correctly. Our ministry advertises courses, and it leads to thousands of positive conversations every month. Some still choose to make negative comments, and I delete them. They used to bother me. Now, I still try to reach out to the negative people with positivity in a private message after deleting their public comment. Some have welcomed my positivity, and it led to Bible studies. Others still try to engage in negativity and give me an opportunity to ignore them. If this seems like too much work and you feel anxious, avoid the social media. It is not a necessary evil if we make the right choices in our approach to social media.

I want to close by giving just a few practical suggestions that have benefited my life in a great way. Most of them have come by using the T.R.I.A.L.S. method, before I even knew it existed.

1. I had been a sports fanatic for over 25 years. I played sports through high school and college. I surrounded myself with people who enjoyed playing and watching sports to the point some of us would talk to a television set. That sounds completely rational, right? I learned watching a football game didn't affect the outcome, not even in a small way. If I enjoy watching just to watch, fantastic. If my favorite team loses and it puts me in a bad mood and causes me stress, I need to learn not to watch or have a different attitude about the game. This is an example of an easy choice to avoid stress.

2. When I was growing up, my mom had a book entitled, *Don't Sweat the Small Stuff and It's All Small Stuff*. I never read the book, but the title has always stuck with me. The proper perspective has always benefited the person who has it. I have been fortunate enough to travel and speak in some of the poorest countries in the world. I have met people who would literally be in pain if they missed a meal because the meals they had were so incredibly small. On occasion, I have fasted for 24 – 48 hours. People who don't eat because they don't have food have a

completely different perspective of food than people who turn down meals because they can or want to lose a few pounds or want to detox or _____.

When I look at the greatest stressors in my life, I try to pause to consider how blessed and fortunate I am to have forms of positivity in my life. When I focus my attention on the positive, everything else seems pretty small.

3. When I was in college, I made some of the best friends. While some friends can cause us stress, others can help us eliminate stress. I remember one occasion when we spent the weekend at one roommate's house. His dad gave us some encouraging words. He related circumstances to a mattress. No one sleeps under a mattress, it isn't comfortable nor is it meant to be slept under. Mattresses can be heavy. We are all dealt different cards. The cards or circumstances in our life are like this mattress. We can choose to lie under them and feel sorry for ourselves because we don't like our circumstances. Or, we can choose to rise above them. We can choose to look at circumstances that are less than ideal and choose to make the best of them. It goes back to our definition of wealth in the chapter on finances. It isn't how much money you make or have that makes you wealthy, it is how you use it.

4. Confidence, competence, communication, and contentment are great tools to help us with stress. I have tried to develop each of these qualities in my daily life. It takes effort. Confidence is seen in many ways, especially in how we carry ourselves and how we look at other people. Competence has to do with the ability to perform the tasks we choose. If an important job is ahead of you, make sure you have the tools and abilities needed before you start. Preparation is key to competence. Communication

has been mentioned in every chapter in this book. Lack of communication gets us in more trouble and causes more stress than any other aspect of our life. The key to overcoming poor communication is good communication. Speak well, listen better. It will pay off. Finally, peace or contentment in life is the opposite of anxiety. Anxiety is what comes from overload of pressure. Contentment comes when we rise above this pressure and enjoy the present circumstances of our life. It is hard, sometimes impossible, to enjoy life when we are never happy with what we have and where we are in life. People who have these qualities choose to have them. People who do not have them choose not to have them.

5. Take time for yourself and don't feel bad about it. Everyone needs to recharge. After a project is complete or you need a break, pick your favorite hobby and take time to enjoy yourself. I love to fish in south Louisiana or compete in a race like Tough Mudder. I do something like this twice each year and never have regrets. Self-love is important.

6. There are so many reasons why anxiety is inevitable. Years ago, I read an interesting story about how monkeys are captured in Africa. The illustration has served me well as I have used it in many lessons. In Africa, people put a small banana inside a jar and tie the jar to a tree or another object and then they hide. A monkey comes along and sees the banana and sticks his hand in the jar and grab the banana. As he tries to pull his hand out, he realizes he cannot get his hand out with the banana in it because his hand becomes too big when his fist is closed around the banana. The monkey begins to pull harder and scream with frustration when he is unable to get the banana out of the jar. This commotion informs the

people who set the trap that they have captured a monkey. As they approach their victim, the monkey can still let go of the banana and run. However, there is something about this banana. He has convinced himself that pulling harder and yelling louder will get the banana out, but it never does. Soon, he finds himself with a bag over his head and complete darkness. His fear causes him to let go of the banana, but it is too late. Like the monkey, we all have the power to let go. We must decide if what we want now is more important than what we want most. If peace is what we want in the present and future, we must let go of whatever it is that prevents us from having it now, even if it's a delicious banana.

I could go on, but the point is all the same. When it comes to anxiety in this life, whether it be marriage, jobs, finances, children, health, or our faith, we need to look inward first. Overcoming anxiety starts with an understanding of what it is and the confidence in knowing we can overcome. We can let go of the banana. We can choose what we hang on to and what we don't. If things are causing us anxiety in life, we need to look for ways to simplify and get rid of what we cannot handle. Let go of the banana!

If you are not someone who relies heavily on a personal relationship with God every single day, I hope the T.R.I.A.L.S. method outlined in this book helps you reduce stress in every area of your life. I would also encourage you to consider finding faith in the creator of this universe. Of all the things you put in your life, God is the only thing that never changes. He will never fail you.

Regardless if you are a person with minimal or a lot of stress in your life, when anxiety seems to grow, stop to ask yourself these six questions and see how T.R.I.A.L.S. can help reduce your stress:

171

1. Am I being transparent?
2. Am I being responsible?
3. Am I being intentional?
4. Am I being appreciative?
5. Am I pushing my limits?
6. Do I need to simplify?

My prayer and my aim is to help as many people as I can live without anxiety. God has helped me to do this in my life without charging me a nickel. I hope reading this book didn't cost you much more than your time and I hope it has helped you overcome anxiety in your life. If it has helped you, I request that you share it with others so that they might benefit as well. May God bless you as you strive to live without stress and anxiety.

Appendix A

My Plan

When it comes to anxiety/stress, I struggle the most with
_____.

T.R.I.A.L.S.

Transparent – Have I been? Am I? Will I be? _____

Responsible – Have I been? Am I? Will I be? _____

Intentional - Have I been? Am I? Will I be? _____

Appreciative - Have I been? Am I? Will I be? _____

Limits – Do I know them? Will I control them? _____

Simplify – Can I? YES!!! Will I? _____

Today, I resolve to be more _____

I will do this by:

_____

_____

God does not want me to live with anxiety. I do not have to live with anxiety. I choose not to live with anxiety.

I will not be anxious for anything, but in everything with prayer and supplication, I will make my requests made known to God so the peace that surpasses all understanding will guard my heart and mind in Christ Jesus.

Works Cited

Aurelius, Marcus. Meditations. Open Road Media, January 27, 2015.

Dyer, Wayne Walter. Your Erroneous Zones. August 1, 1976.

Kiyosaki, Robert and Lechter, Sharon. Rich Kid, Smart Kid, 2001.

Lewis, C.S. The Magician's Nephew. May 2, 1955.

Maxwell, John. Breaking the Patterns of Worry for Your Team. June 11, 2011.

Stanley, Andy. Deep and Wide, September 25, 2012.

Turner, Kristen. The Simple Vida, August 2018.

Turner, Timothy. Preaching to a Programmed People. 1995.

The Holy Bible – New American Standard Version, 1963.

Barna Research Group. https://www.barna.com/research/porn-in-the-digital-age-new-research-reveals-10-trends/. April6, 2016.

Olson, Samantha. March 8, 2015. https://www.medicaldaily.com/how-3-meals-day-became-rule-and-why-we-should-be-eating-whenever-we-get-hungry-324892

Saul, Heather. https://www.independent.co.uk/news/people/why-mark-zuckerberg-wears-the-same-clothes-to-work-everyday-a6834161.html

American Psychology Association - http://www.apa.org/

www.pewinternet.org

Webster, Merriam. https://www.merriam-webster.com/

Suggested Readings

Chapman, Gary. The Five Love Languages. 1995.

Chapman, Gary. The Five Love Languages of Children. 1997

Sinek, Simon. Start with Why.

Turansky, Scott and Miller, Joann. Good and Angry: Exchanging Frustration for Character in You and Your Kids! 2002.

Suggested Podcasts and Blogs

https://www.celebratecalm.com/

blog.johnmaxwell.com/blog

Check out my website:

http://trialsbook.com/

Follow the Trials Book On Facebook:

https://www.facebook.com/Trials-Book-107049794072637/

Join The Facebook Group Today!

https://www.facebook.com/groups/563843334425747/

Tell others about the book by leaving a review on Amazon:

https://www.amazon.com/T-R-I-L-S-Journey-Anxiety-Peace-ebook/dp/B07ZQZDJKW/ref=sr_1_1?keywords=chase+turner&qid=1576868009&sr=8-1

To order a printed copy or the eBook, scan the QR code below:

P. 22 " STRESSFUL ARE NOT USUALLY HAPPY PEOPLE AND HAPPY PEOPLE ARE NOT USUALLY STRESSED OUT. IT IS HARD TO BE BOTH AT THE SAME TIME.

Made in the USA
San Bernardino, CA
27 February 2020